THE RESPONSE TO INDUSTRIALISM
1885–1914

The Response to

THE CHICAGO HISTORY OF AMERICAN CIVILIZATION

Daniel J. Boorstin, EDITOR

Industrialism: 1885-1914

By Samuel P. Hays

 THE UNIVERSITY OF CHICAGO PRESS
CHICAGO AND LONDON

THE UNIVERSITY OF CHICAGO PRESS, CHICAGO 60637
The University of Chicago Press, Ltd., London

81 80   19 18 17 16

ISBN: 0–226–32161–4 (clothbound); 0–226–32162–2 (paperbound)
Library of Congress Catalog Card Number: 57–6981

For

MY MOTHER AND FATHER

Editor's Preface

The "in-between" ages, when great events were supposedly not happening but only being prepared, have been the happy hunting grounds of historians who would make the past nothing but a conflict of impersonal forces. The period from the end of Reconstruction to the outbreak of World War I has too often been described as if individual human beings had gone underground and the national scene had been taken over by vast economic movements. The lack of dramatic focus in this period has tempted historians to treat it abstractly, as if Americans did not resume their individual lives until another war aroused them.

But for Mr. Hays the years from 1885 to 1914 are marked by varied and intense human responses. For him, economic development and social conflict in these years provide the historical setting in which different groups of Americans encountered their own particular problems. Because the tides of change reach back into Reconstruction and the Civil War and flow forward into the Wilsonian era, he cannot cut off his period as neatly as if he were recounting an armed conflict.

By starting with groups of individuals and seeing where and how they were situated, and what they wanted or thought they wanted,

Editor's Preface

Mr. Hays avoids presenting the age as a conflict merely between "haves" and "have-nots." The typically American variety of these groups, together with their continuing geographic and social fluidity, prevented the hardening and sharpening of class lines. This helps explain why few Americans sought refuge in ideologies like those which had congealed in many European countries during comparable eras of industrialism. What Professor Hays describes, then, is not simply "the response to industrialism" but a peculiarly American response, which in its very inconsistency and inarticulateness was to account for salient features of American politics in our times.

In drawing on the rich storehouse of recent scholarship to offer the general reader a vigorous interpretation of a complex age, Mr. Hays serves well the purpose of the "Chicago History of American Civilization." The series contains two kinds of books. A *chronological* group, of which this volume is a part, will provide a coherent narrative of American history from its beginning to the present day. A *topical* group will deal with the history of varied and important aspects of American life. Those which have already been published are listed at the end of this volume.

DANIEL J. BOORSTIN

Table of Contents

The Old and the New

The history of modern America is, above all, a story of the impact of industrialism on every phase of human life. It is difficult for us today fully to imagine the implications of this change, for we did not know an earlier America firsthand. But the American of 1914 could contrast, in his own experience, the old with the new. Looking backward scarcely more than forty or fifty years, he fully recognized that his country had changed rapidly and fundamentally. He had personally experienced the transition from a society relatively untouched by industrialism to one almost transformed by it. Seldom, if ever, in American history had so much been altered within the lifetime of a single man.

Had he been a manufacturer, a merchant, a laborer, or a farmer, the American of 1914 would have experienced the transition from relatively stable, local business affairs to intense nationwide competition that rendered his way of making a living far less secure. Formerly, perhaps, he had resided in the intimate surroundings of his town or rural community. If he remained there in 1914, he had encountered with some fear the expansion into the countryside of a new urban culture that threatened the familiar order with strange, even dangerous, ideas. Or, moving to Chicago, one of the nation's rapidly growing urban centers, he had experienced the indifference of city people toward each other, which contrasted sharply with the atmosphere of the small community from which he had come. On the streets he had met newcomers from foreign nations, speaking a language he had never heard and celebrating holidays he had never known. Had he come from abroad as an immigrant, he would have faced a strange, new land where the people were often hostile and frequently objected when he tried to re-establish here his old-country ways of life. If he had been especially sensitive to personal values, he would have looked with horror upon the way in which the impersonal forces of industrialism seemed to place one at the mercy of influences far beyond one's control. In such an atmosphere how could personal character count for anything; how could anyone exercise personal responsibility?

Behind these changes that the American of 1914 had experienced in his own lifetime lay a new factory-machine method of production, with its specialized tasks, its large aggregations of capital, and its advancing technology. Destroying local and separate activities, the new forms of transportation and communication linked more tightly every group and section into one interdependent nation. Eager to use their capital, their skills, and their cunning for economic gain, millions of people from Europe and rural America poured into the metropolitan nerve centers of the new economic order. The American people subordinated religion, education, and politics to the process of creating wealth. Increasing production, employment, and income became the measures of community success, and personal riches the mark of individual achievement.

By the time of World War I, few activities of the American people remained uninfluenced by industrialism. Whether one had sought to enhance his social prestige, to preserve his pattern of culture, to express his religious beliefs, or to gain material success, he had been forced to contend with the vast changes swirling about him. Industrialism provided for every American an opportunity to participate in great economic achievements and to enjoy a higher standard of living; but it also demanded drastic changes in their lives. It forced upon every one a new atmosphere, a new setting, to which he had to adjust in his thought, play, worship, and work. Although the citizen of 1914 might be most concerned with spiritual affairs and inward personal growth, as many were, he could not afford to ignore either the decline of interest in religion or those consequences of industrialism which hampered creative expression. If material gain was his motive, he could hardly succeed without fully taking into account the rapidly changing facts of economic life.

The variety of ways in which the people of the United States responded to these drastic innovations is the subject of this book. We shall examine how the circumstances of life were modified for different groups of people; how, in response, they altered or failed to alter their activities; how they joined with each other to cope with a new, impersonal economic environment; and how they struggled, almost frantically, to preserve ways of life they felt were threatened. This period, the Populist-Progressive Era, is one of the richest in American history, for here one can observe changes in the experience and behavior of people under the impact of the most profound influence in the modern world. Industrialism opened vistas of vast human achievement; yet it produced a restless and strife-torn society and gave rise to nostalgia for a calmer, less perplexed, pre-industrial life. This is a story of human adjustment, of the ways in which Americans worked out their lives in a swiftly moving industrial age.

I. Industrialism Under Way

To the uncritical observer, the record of industrialism has been written in the production statistics, the accomplishments of inventor-heroes, and the rising standard of living of the American people. Even more significant, however, were the less obvious and the less concrete changes: the expansion of economic relationships from personal contacts within a village community to impersonal forces in the nation and the entire world; the standardization of life accompanying the standardization of goods and of methods of production; increasing specialization in occupations with the resulting dependence of people upon each other to satisfy their wants; a feeling of insecurity as men faced vast and rapidly changing economic forces that they could not control; the decline of interest in nonmaterial affairs and the rise of the acquisition of material wealth as the major goal in life. These intangible innovations deeply affected the American people; here lay the real human drama of the new age.

THE TRANSPORTATION AND COMMUNICATIONS REVOLUTION

In the United States in the nineteenth century many factors favored industrial growth. Abundant resources, high in quality and exploitable with relatively small amounts of labor and capital, lay waiting to be developed. Industry could draw a large and cheap labor supply from a reservoir of peasants in Europe who eagerly responded when they learned of American economic opportunities. Domestic capital, derived from earlier mercantile enterprise, provided funds essential for the nation's internal development; European capital augmented domestic savings especially in mining, railroads, and banks. Enterprisers in the United States, moreover, faced few political barriers to economic exchange; the Constitution prohibited states from imposing restrictions on interstate commerce and thereby promoted combination of the factors of production over a vast and varied geographical area. Finally, pre-industrial America had developed a capable group of entrepreneurs; though experienced chiefly in organizing commerce, they were eager to take advantage of every opportunity to expand their operations. The American people displayed a vigorous spirit of enterprise notably in the North, which boasted of its "Yankee ingenuity."

A nationwide transportation system constructed between 1820 and 1915 enabled Americans to exploit fully these latent factors of economic growth. The success of the Erie Canal in New York and the development of the steamboat set off a craze of canal building in the 1820's and initiated a revolution in transportation and communication. Railroads, first constructed in the 1830's, soon surpassed the canals in importance. Although slowed momentarily by the Civil War, railroad expansion proceeded with great rapidity between 1868 and the depression of 1893. Construction was limited to the area east of the Mississippi prior to the Civil War but expanded to the Pacific Coast in the 1870's and 1880's. In the industrial Northeast new mileage produced an extremely dense and complex network. By 1915, when the railroads boasted some 250,000 miles of track, not an important community in the country lay outside this extensive system.

Railroad mileage grew rapidly because Americans in all walks of life visualized the economic progress that cheap transportation could set in motion. Merchants in thriving communities and in communities which hoped to thrive endeavored to reach wider markets by extending their transportation facilities. Before the Civil War, merchants of each of the major Atlantic seaports—New York, Boston, Philadelphia, and Baltimore—promoted competitive railroad building to tap the interior Ohio Valley. The search for markets generated hundreds of similar projects throughout the country. Frequently they were financed through bond and stock subscriptions raised either from merchants themselves or from the general public in campaigns which local commercial associations promoted. Farmers eagerly joined in the crusade; they, too, contributed personal savings and often mortgaged their farms to raise funds to speed construction. Whole communities, realizing that the key to economic growth lay in transportation, participated in the mania. When the town of Ithaca, New York, for example, bonded itself for funds to construct a railroad, the local editor exclaimed, "There is no reason why the direct route from San Francisco to New York may not be through Ithaca." Such enthusiasts visualized new industry, new jobs, better markets, and rising property values that canals and railroads would create. Although these visions were often unrealistic, transportation promoters were not inclined to discourage them.

Cheap, rapid transportation brought all sectors of the economy into close contact with one another; factors of production could be combined far more readily than before. Previously, for example, high shipment costs often prohibited the combination of iron ore and coal located scarcely ten miles apart; but now the economic distance between such resources was phenomenally reduced. Canals and steamboats lowered river-transport costs to less than a tenth of land travel. Initially railroads did not lower rates further between points served by waterways; but they were faster than steamboats, were free from ice and low-water barriers, and penetrated to areas which water carriers could not possibly reach.

These efficiencies stimulated economic growth not only by reducing the cost of production but even more significantly by creating a national market; the transportation and communications revolution destroyed barriers to distribution and permitted producers to sell to consumers throughout the nation. For example, the local blacksmith's plowshares, kettles, pots, and pans before the transportation revolution cost less than similar items manufactured fifty miles away and subject to high shipping charges. Manufacturers were excluded from every distant market, but within their own locality enjoyed a monopoly. Railroads in particular now eliminated these exclusive markets; they opened every part of the country to the products of modern industry and by stimulating mass consumption greatly encouraged the growth of mass production.

No less important in accelerating the tempo of economic life was rapid nationwide communication. The telegraph was first successfully operated in 1844 by Samuel F. B. Morse (1791–1872), a New England artist turned inventor. Widely used during the Civil War, it co-ordinated the myriad transactions of a growing economy as effectively as it had aided military operations. While the telegraph speeded communications over longer distances, the telephone, patented by Alexander Graham Bell (1847–1922) in 1876, replaced messengers in the mushrooming urban centers and speeded the complex administrative processes necessary for large-scale industrial management. The modern press, though less spectacular, was equally vital in co-ordinating the intricate functions of the new economy. Technical innovations, such as the rotary press (1875), enormously increased the output and lowered the cost of newspaper production. Nationwide advertising, which appeared first in the religious journals, the most widely circulated magazines of the day, brought producer and consumer together with a speed previously impossible. The new communication supplemented the new transportation in creating the highly integrated and complex human relationships inherent in modern industrialism.

Railroad construction in the latter half of the nineteenth century served as the most important direct stimulant to production. Lumber mills, quarries, ironworks, and carriage factories found a rapidly growing market in railways. The railroad-construction labor force reached 200,000 in the boom of the 1880's. The new roads, moreover, were major users of both domestic and foreign capital. The close correspondence between the ups and downs of new construction and nationwide economic fluctuations in the post–Civil War era provided evidence of the all-pervasive impact of the railroad on the entire economy. A loss of confidence in railroads affected the money market so as to trigger the depressions of 1873, 1884, and 1893.

The rapidly expanding iron and steel industry, stimulated enormously by the railroads, became the foundation of industrial America. Far outstripping the domestic supply, the need for iron and steel constantly encouraged expansion of American mills. By 1850 railroads had become the leading industrial market for iron, and by 1875 railroad construction, reconstruction, and maintenance consumed over half of the iron produced in the United States. The demand for railroad iron, moreover, brought about the all-important technological shift from charcoal to coke in iron production. Before the introduction of the steam locomotive, rural blacksmiths, who purchased most of the iron, preferred a charcoal-manufactured product which they could work more easily than iron smelted with coal. Coal-smelted iron was quite satisfactory for structural shapes, rails, and locomotives. Coke-produced iron, moreover, permitted a mass production of iron previously not practical. The heavy cost of transportating wood for charcoal limited the size of the area from which fuel could be feasibly drawn, and consequently the size of the blast furnace. But the enormous coal fields of western Pennsylvania presented no such limitations; in a relatively small geographical area they provided the fuel essential for large-scale production. Once the new railroad market appeared, therefore, coke replaced charcoal, and huge blast furnaces and rolling mills grew rapidly in the new capital of the iron industry at Pittsburgh.

A number of farsighted entrepreneurs, most notably Andrew Carnegie (1835–1919), a Scotch immigrant who rose from bobbin-boy to steel magnate in seventeen years, rapidly expanded iron and steel production both in size and in technique. The Carnegie steel-works catered to the railroad industry. Carnegie, who was widely known for his ability as a salesman, cultivated the personal friendship of railroad executives and obtained heavy orders for rails, bridge steel, and other structural shapes. He led the way in organizing a vertically integrated iron and steel business. By combining in one organization the major elements of the industry he rapidly reduced the costs of production. After bringing into his enterprise Henry Clay Frick, who owned immense deposits of coking coal in western Pennsylvania, Carnegie acquired a heavy interest in the rich Lake Superior iron-ore area and purchased a fleet of carriers to bring the ore across the Great Lakes to Lake Erie ports.

Railroads, then, both lowered the cost of transportation and stimulated the economy directly by their use of labor, capital, and iron. They also created the mass markets that made mass production possible. When markets were local and limited in size, there was

9

no incentive for businessmen to produce in larger amounts to realize the resultant savings in costs. But the unlimited possibilities of the new mass markets stimulated entrepreneurs to explore and develop mass-production techniques. In the iron and steel industry, for example, the size and scope of production increased rapidly: the average daily output of a blast furnace increased from no more than 45 tons before the Civil War to more than 400 tons in the early twentieth century. Mass production was introduced in many other fields as well, notably lumbering, flour milling, meat packing, and textile manufacturing. For example, larger and more efficient saws were adopted in the lumber industry, and in the milling industry the rolling process, first used extensively in Minneapolis, increased both the output and the quality of flour.

Mass production also depended upon improved techniques, or which standardization of parts and processes was especially significant. Repetitive production of a standard item, independent of the vagaries of the individual craftsman, was the heart of the technical revolution. Each product had to be assembled from a given number of parts, any one of which could be replaced by an identical part. This method of manufacture was developed first in the production of guns in the early nineteenth century by Eli Whitney (1765–1825), a New Englander who earlier had invented the cotton gin (1793) while studying law in Georgia. Others soon applied the principle of interchangeable parts to clocks, sewing machines, typewriters, and many other items. The success of this innovation depended on exact measurement, provided by the vernier caliper, which was first made in the United States in 1851. Subsequent improvements of this device made it possible in the twentieth century to measure one ten-thousandth of an inch. At first limited to the mass production of parts, standardization soon invaded the process of assembling parts into finished products. Frederick Taylor (1856–

1915), for example, undertook extensive time-and-motion studies to provide the basic data for standardizing assembly methods in factories. Coming from a well-to-do Philadelphia family, Taylor gave up the study of law at Harvard to become an apprentice machinist at the age of nineteen. Fourteen years later, after rising from laborer to chief engineer of the Midvale Steel Company, he organized his own firm to sell to manufacturers the idea of "scientific management," which involved techniques to promote efficiency not only in the shop but also in the office and in the accounting and sales departments. New assembly methods were first used dramatically by Henry Ford (1863–1947), who established the assembly line, or "progressive line production," in the automobile industry in 1914.

The rapid growth of the American economy depended also on an increasing specialization and division of labor. Relatively independent Jacks-of-all-trades (village blacksmiths, for example) gave way to many interdependent individuals skilled in particular economic activities. Most striking was the separation of labor and management functions, which arose slowly in agriculture but rapidly in industry. Specialized managers and specialized wage earners replaced semi-independent artisans; manual laborers no longer organized production or sold finished products. Specialized retailing replaced the general store; the jobber concentrated increasingly on a particular line of goods; investment bankers who floated stocks and bonds became separated from commercial bankers who made loans to business. The sole link among these specialists lay in the price-and-market system in which impersonal monetary values governed the relationships between buyers and sellers of labor, commodities, and credit. Those at the core of this price-and-market network, such as capitalists and business managers, possessed great power to manipulate it, while farmers and wage earners, far less capable of influencing large economic affairs, were more frequently

manipulated by others. Thus, the closely knit economy of specialists gave rise to a division between dominant and subordinate,
central and peripheral, economic roles.

A simpler distribution system, involving fewer middlemen and
more direct buying and selling, replaced the innumerable traders
formerly required. Previously manufacturers had sold almost exclusively to jobbers who stocked the goods of many different makers
and forwarded them in turn to wholesalers. This system was defec-
tive for manufacturers: jobbers hesitated to push any particular line
of goods, but manufacturers were eager to exploit the possibilities
of a national market by rapidly expanding sales of their own goods.
Manufacturers took over more and more of the process of distribution. In 1896, for example, the Pittsburgh Plate Glass Company,
dissatisfied with the practices of its jobbers, established a chain of
warehouses throughout the country to distribute its own products.
Such firms, bypassing jobbers, sold directly to regional wholesalers
and often to retailers as well as to industrial and institutional buyers.
They developed active sales departments, spent increasing sums for
advertising, and registered brand names at the Patent Office in order to distinguish their products from other standard, mass-produced items. Traveling salesmen now represented the producer, and
Rural Free Delivery (1896) and Parcel Post (1913) enabled manufacturers to sell to farmers without middlemen. Such innovations in
mass retailing as the Sears-Roebuck and Montgomery Ward mail-
order houses, the chains, and the department store, which often purchased directly from manufacturers, also contributed to a simpler
and more efficient distribution system.

Changes in grain marketing dramatically illustrated the manner
in which distribution became more efficient. Marketing facilities in
Chicago, the new center of the grain trade, could not handle the
immense amounts of wheat which railroads poured into the city

from the Middle West in the 1850's and 1860's. A revolution in grain handling resulted. Wheat, formerly transported in bags and carried from railroad to lake vessel on human shoulders, now was shipped bulk in freight cars, dumped into endless chain-buckets, carried to the top of huge elevators, and dropped into ships. The savings in labor and the consequent decline in distribution costs were enormous. The entire system of transporting grain from the Middle West to European markets became equally streamlined. Thus there developed a unified national grain-marketing system in which Chicago commodity merchants played a key role.

COMMERCIAL AGRICULTURE

The tighter national and even international distribution network that linked grain producer and grain consumer symbolized the radical change which the transportation and communications revolution had created in agriculture. Formerly farmers had remained comparatively self-sufficient, producing much of their own food, clothing, furniture, and equipment. But just as the new national market destroyed the local blacksmith in the face of mass-produced hardware, no less did it outmode production by the farmer's wife in competition with the clothing manufacturer. Household industry remained longest in those areas which high-cost transportation rendered least accessible to the outside world and therefore where consumers were least able to purchase factory-made goods. The same revolution in transport, opening up new markets for the farmer, enabled him to earn more cash to purchase manufactured products. Subsistence farming, in other words, gave way to commercial farming. Instead of producing most of the items needed for his livelihood, the farmer became a specialist, concentrating on those crops that climate, soil, and ability enabled him to produce most profitably.

Technology contributed to this transformation. John Deere

(1804–86), an Illinois blacksmith, began to produce a steel plow at Moline in 1847; it proved to be far superior to wooden and cast-iron plows in turning the tough virgin sods of the Middle West and rapidly reduced the cost of soil preparation. Even more spectacular were improvements in harvesting: the reaper, developed by Cyrus H. McCormick (1809–84) in the Middle West; the self-binder, which cut the grain and tied it into sheaves; and finally the huge combines, used on the broad wheat fields of the Red River Valley of the North and of the Central Valley of California, which joined reaping and threshing in one operation powered by steam engines. Between 1830 and 1896 these new implements almost cut in half the time and labor cost of production for all crops; for wheat it reduced the time worked to one-twentieth that required for hand labor, and the labor cost to a fifth of the previous figure. But this machinery also increased the capital investment required for farming. Whereas in 1820 a farmer could buy adequate equipment for an average, well-managed family farm for $100, by 1900 a sum of $750 was needed, even though the price of farm machinery had declined sharply after 1880. Readily available capital funds became increasingly essential for agricultural enterprise and yet were frequently difficult to secure.

Cereal-growing farmers in the Middle and Far West adopted harvesting and threshing machinery during and soon after the Civil War. Southern and eastern crops, on the other hand, did not lend themselves to machine methods. The harvest of southern cotton and tobacco required careful hand labor, as did most operations in eastern truck, dairy, and fruit farming. The principal innovations in eastern agriculture consisted less in the use of machinery to replace manual operations and more in intensive scientific management: specialized dairy cattle breeding, insect and disease control, fertilizer, improved plant varieties, and new methods of preserving perishables. Three notable advances came in dairying: the DeLaval cream separator in 1878, a test for butterfat content perfected in 1890 by Dr. Stephen Babcock at the Wisconsin experiment station, and later in the twentieth century the milking machine. Yet considerable hand labor continued to be required even in dairying.

Markets, machinery, and science, then, transformed American agriculture from a relatively simple operation, requiring little capital and less knowledge, into a highly complex affair, demanding increasing amounts of investment, equipment, scientific information, and close attention to markets. The farmer was now irrevocably entwined in the complex industrial system. Not as a Jack-of-all-trades, but only as a calculating, alert, and informed businessman, could he survive.

GEOGRAPHICAL SPECIALIZATION

Within this general pattern of economic change occurred considerable geographical specialization. Industry became concentrated north of the Ohio River and east of the Mississippi. Here were the new iron and steel mills, the textile and shoe factories, the lumber mills and furniture establishments, and hundreds of other firms; here was the densest railroad network in the country. A rich store of readily available resources, such as Pennsylvania coal, Middle Atlantic and Great Lakes lumber, and New England water-power, partly determined this location of industry. In addition, the area's natural arteries provided the earliest and cheapest east-west transportation route. The Erie Canal, which penetrated the Appalachian chain at its lowest gap, linked the East with the Great Lakes. Railroads followed patterns that these earlier forms of transportation established. But the location of industry was influenced as well by the already existing concentration of commercial activity in the northeastern seaports of Boston, New York, Philadelphia, and Baltimore. Industry was attracted to these older urban centers because they were at the hub of growing transportation systems and because capital accumulated in commerce, as well as an adequate labor force, was more readily available there than elsewhere.

The South and the West, predominantly agricultural and mining areas, served as markets for northeastern products and as sources of its food and raw materials. Cotton, tobacco, and rice from the South, grain from the Middle West and the Pacific Coast, and beef from the Great Plains were carried to urban markets in the Northeast and in Europe. The primary processors of farm products migrated to these producing areas. As grain production shifted west from the Middle Atlantic states, so did flour milling—to St. Louis, then to Minneapolis and Kansas City. As beef and pork production moved to the western Middle West, the slaughtering capital of the nation shifted from Cincinnati to Chicago and finally to a half-dozen cities, such as Kansas City and Sioux City, on the edge of the cattle country. The West also shipped industrial raw materials eastward. Iron from the Lake Superior region, copper from the same area and later from Montana, Arizona, and Utah, lead and zinc from the Kansas-Missouri-Arkansas section, and lumber from the Pacific Northwest all contributed their share of the ingredients of northeastern industry. Little manufacturing developed in the West and the South save in a few specialized areas; those regions depended on the Northeast for their manufactured products, their clothing, hardware, farm machinery, and construction materials. Thus emerged a regional division of labor which the transportation network bound into a national economic system.

Within each geographical region, specialization between rural and urban areas grew rapidly. The city, the center of industrial activity, concentrated on producing manufactured goods, performing far more effectively functions that farmers had formerly undertaken. Rural areas, on the other hand, retained their specialty, food production. Cities served as the nerve centers of the new economy. To them came labor, capital, and raw materials; from them finished products were dispensed. They became great shipping points, manufacturing centers, and accumulations of capital, skill, and managerial ability. The core of the city was business, around which other human activities arose to fashion a social and cultural as well as an economic community. These industrial cities attracted millions of people from abroad and from the American countryside. The European newcomers arrived in waves that coincided roughly with the rise and fall of the nation's level of economic activity. An equally large number of people migrated from rural areas to the cities, especially in the industrial Northeast. Less prosperous farmers in that area, unable to meet western competition, sought their fortunes in the new urban centers. With the influx of population, industrial cities mushroomed beyond their original limits to become vast metropolitan centers.

GOVERNMENT AND ECONOMIC GROWTH

The drive to create wealth, which underlay these transformations, pervaded political institutions as well; for American political life, through its representative government, has reflected constantly the attitudes of the American people. In these decades of industrial growth politics and government were called upon to be the instruments of material progress. No doctrinaire view prevailed as to the proper role of government in economic life. There was only the pragmatic assumption that the business of America was to create wealth and that government at all levels should contribute to this task. At times some leaders and groups pretended to believe in laissez faire, but they did not hesitate to take advantage of government when they found it useful to their own particular method of creating wealth. The American economy involved a mixture of public and private stimulants, federal, state, and local assistance for capital, technical advice, generous tax concessions, and the use of legal power to lessen the rigors of competition. Such aid, often given in the absence of private resources, frequently ceased as private initiative supplied the deficiency, but the creators of wealth demanded that government stand prepared to assist when needed.

The nation's transportation companies, for example, received considerable public financial aid. In 1862 the federal government provided the first of a number of land grants to encourage construction of transcontinental railroads. The original grant went to the Union Pacific; eventually over a dozen lines received some 158,-000,000 acres, of which they secured final patents for 130,000,000 acres. The roads sold some of this land to obtain capital; the remainder they offered as security for privately raised funds. But federal grants were only the more spectacular form of aid. Even in the 1850's the states had granted public lands, received from the federal government, to companies constructing railroads within their borders. The peak of state capital contributions to transportation came in the canal era. When taxpayers discovered that they had committed themselves to high taxes to pay for projects that did not return expected high profits, they obtained state constitutional prohibitions against public appropriations for internal improvements. Thereupon counties and municipalities became an important source of financing. Public aid, save in the South, was not large as compared with private funds, but it provided critically important capital to begin or complete projects for which private financing did not appear.

Less spectacular, though equally far-reaching, was public assistance to scientific agriculture; in fact, the federal government soon became, as it is today, the main promoter of agricultural research.

Industrialism under Way

In the Morrill Act (1862), Congress provided land grants to the states as capital funds for agricultural and mechanical colleges, and in the Second Morrill Act (1890) the government began a program of annual financial aid to these institutions. After a few states had established agricultural experiment stations to encourage agricultural research, Congress in the Hatch Act (1887) provided funds to launch a nationwide system of such centers. The Department of Agriculture, established in 1862, achieved full cabinet rank in 1889; its scientific activities grew, as bureau after bureau arose to deal with such subjects as plant chemistry, entomology, plant disease, and forestry. Government clearly was the only force that could promote agricultural science; to the organized agricultural societies of the time it seemed logical that public enterprise should contribute in this way to private endeavor.

The tariff became a far more controversial public stimulant to the economy. American industries subject to competition from imports took refuge in the tariff as a means of protecting the domestic market for their products. In 1861, after two decades of low duties, the Republicans had re-established an avowedly protective system by enacting the Morrill Tariff. Thereafter, through such Republican-sponsored measures as the McKinley Act of 1890, the Dingley Act of 1897, and the Payne-Aldrich Act of 1909, Congress raised duties and added new products to the list of protected items. But although the tariff stimulated some lines of production, it retarded others. Congress found it especially difficult to protect both manufactured items and raw materials; industries which demanded protection for their finished products insisted equally on free entry for their supplies. In the mid-1880's a movement arose in industrial New England, which was deficient in coal, iron, and other natural resources, to place such items on the free list. Raw-material producers rose in protest and successfully squelched the proposal.

The Response to Industrialism

The economic growth of the post–Civil War era took place in an atmosphere of speculation, waste, and disorder. Americans, convinced that their natural resources were unlimited, took little care to save or renew them. Confident that the value of property would rise in the course of rapid growth, every property holder became a speculator, fondly hoping to make a capital gain, to sell at a figure far above the purchase price. Each enterpriser rushed to obtain his share of the markets and productive possibilities suddenly created. It was a field day for the promoter, the individual who visualized opportunities not in continuous profits from a stable enterprise but in the original profits of creating new enterprise. Charles R. Flint (1850–1934), for example, widely known as the "father of the trusts," organized a score of industrial consolidations, including the United States Rubber Company and the predecessor of the International Business Machines Corporation. Landowners promoted towns that would, they said, outshine El Dorado; townspeople promoted transportation that would, they said, make their village the hub of the universe; and investment bankers promoted business consolidations that would, they said, establish one corporation as the emperor of business. Optimism as to the unlimited future persuaded enterprisers on every hand to pay dearly those who would set economic activity in motion.

The desire to create wealth possessed all Americans. It was not only rich men or great corporation presidents who exploited resources or speculated in property. The farmer who purchased one hundred and sixty acres from a railroad or obtained it free from the government under the Homestead Act (1862) hoped as eagerly for an increase in values as did the land agent who acquired fifty thousand acres of fine timber. Far more important than differences in the size of their holdings was the common desire of all to profit from the rising price of land. Frequently the man with less property complained of the speculative propensities of the "large corporations," but such arguments usually arose from jealousy rather than from a fundamental difference in attitude. The man of small means, moreover, exploited natural resources as eagerly as did the corporate owners; neither looked upon soil, forests, or minerals as limited, and neither wished to pay the increasing costs of more prudent resource management. Only a small number grew rich from profits from the rise in values, but few failed to grasp the opportunity when it came their way.

Not many enterprisers felt compelled to behave so as to retain the confidence and trust of their associates and the public. The rush to secure as large a share as possible of the new markets gave rise to sharp competitive practices. The Standard Oil Company, for example, received from railroads not only rebates on its shipments, a common practice, but a percentage of the shipping charges paid by its competitors as well. Such practices, soon condemned as "unfair," were often illegal. Both large and small entrepreneurs constantly sought ways of evading the spirit of hampering laws. Tempted by unregulated stock exchanges and by the reservoirs of capital in the new corporate form of business organization, many directors could not resist manipulating securities for personal gain at the expense of stockholders. The notorious Jim Fisk and Jay Gould, after joining with Daniel Drew to fleece the Erie Railroad, almost cornered the New York gold supply for their own personal profit. Such men did not hesitate to bribe whole legislatures to obtain laws essential to carry out their aims. The New York lawmakers responded readily to the interests of Fisk, Gould, and Drew, and on the national level the Grant administration seemed extraordinarily close to the operations of a great number of economic freebooters. These were only extreme examples of the instability in both public and private relations fostered by the rush to take advantage of the new opportunities to create wealth.

In industrial America material success became the predominant measure of human achievement; the very term "success" implied material prosperity. Businessmen rather than politicians and theologians now commanded primary prestige. Steel magnate Andrew Carnegie argued that men of talent and ability should not enter politics, which seemed to him a relatively unimportant activity, but should instead go into business. Most Americans agreed by pronouncing politics an ignoble profession, fit only for those who failed at economic enterprise. Although few young people trained themselves for a career in politics, it was not long before many prepared for a career in business. The public avidly read Horatio Alger's (1834–99) stories of men who had risen from rags to riches and William Makepeace Thayer's (1820–98) guides to success. Orison Swett Marden argued in *Pushing to the Front* (1894) that the major element in success was the will to succeed; his book went through two hundred and fifty editions. In 1897, Marden, who had lost his first fortune in the depression of 1893, began to publish a magazine named *Success*. Winning a wide audience, *Success* prospered until it failed in 1912, after having helped to bring its publisher both wealth and fame.

The industrial invasion of American culture drastically affected the nature and role of religion in American life. Religion increasingly lost prestige, so that it came to be reserved for one morning weekly. Theology, thought about the nature of God and man, and ideas about morality attracted less interest than ever before. The times preferred a religion of action—Josiah Strong (1847–1916) called it *spiritual* Christianity—a religion that would prompt men to feel and to act rather than to think. On the other hand, Christianity frequently came to be a religion that justified the creation and acquisition of wealth, thus keeping in tune with the materialistic temper of America. Outspoken religious leaders of the day firmly argued that material success provided outward evidence of an inward moral and religious character. In fact, Russell Conwell (1843–1925) argued in his oft-repeated lecture, "Acres of Diamonds," that to make money honestly was both a Christian obligation and a form of preaching the gospel.

Industrialism, then, pervaded every segment and every activity of American life. How would Americans respond to these transformations? How would farmers adjust to the commercial and financial network in which they were now entwined? How would they react to the penetration of an urban way of life into their predominantly rural culture? Would workers readily accept their new role as wage earners in place of their former semi-independent artisan position? Would the South and the West remain content in an economic condition subordinate to the Northeast? Would the new urban inhabitants be able to fashion an effective community life amid people from such diverse backgrounds? How would native Americans respond to the newcomers? Would the all-absorbing material ambitions of the new society be approved without criticism? And would the American people call upon their government to help them cope effectively with the problems that industrialism created? In short, would the nation wholeheartedly accept the implications of the industrial age or react adversely to them? The way in which Americans responded to industrial change is the dominant theme of the Populist-Progressive period in American history and the subject of the remaining chapters of this book.

II. The Shock of Change

To most Americans the adjustment to industrialism came slowly and painfully. Incredulous at the scope and intensity of innovation, they resisted economic change, often attributing its dislocations to the evil actions of a few designing men rather than to broad changes in society. Many Americans drew back in disgust before the crudeness of the new age and the graft, corruption, praise of material values, and destruction of resources which accompanied it. The more affluent found it difficult to believe that social unrest could abound in a nation rich with natural wealth and opportunities; some of them argued that to achieve progress many would have to be poor, others that discontent should be suppressed by force. Labor and agriculture, convinced that the new organization of economic life was simply a selfish capitalist trick which could be undone, sought to destroy the network of impersonal economic relations in which they had become enmeshed. The last third of the nineteenth century was an era of popular schemes for remaking society, of simple solutions to complex problems, of endeavors to escape from industrial innovation rather than to come to grips with it.

The Shock of Change

The United States, wrote E. L. Godkin in the *Nation* in 1866, is a "gaudy stream of bespangled, belaced, and beruffled barbarians. . . . Who knows how to be rich in America? Plenty of people know how to get money; but . . . to be rich properly is, indeed, a fine art. It requires culture, imagination, and character." Godkin spoke for a host of Americans who stood aghast at what they called the materialism, the barbarism and immorality that had taken root in their country. These critics were concentrated mainly in New England but appeared throughout the country. They were patricians; they came from the "best families," families with inherited wealth, tradition, leisure, and education, who were not intimately involved in the great industrial barbecue. They looked down upon the mad scene below, alarmed especially that the men of new wealth, who lacked the "restraints of culture, experience, the pride, or even the inherited caution of class or rank," now occupied positions of prestige and influence. They became convinced that ideals, character, and moral values were fast disappearing from American civilization.

The Gilded Age was especially disturbing to creative writers. Those who carried forward the "genteel tradition" in poetry and fiction reasserted the value of good manners, character, and strict moral behavior, qualities which they felt were under attack. A number of editors, Thomas Bailey Aldrich of the *Atlantic* and Richard Watson Gilder of the *Century*, for example, put before their public works of poetry, fiction, and drama that idealized life. Henry James (1843–1916), though able in his novels and short stories to view his own predicament objectively, fled to England, where he discovered a more congenial atmosphere. Henry Adams (1838–1913), on the other hand, turned to history; in *Mont-Saint-Michel and Chartres* (1904) he found satisfaction in a medieval society which he depicted as exalting spiritual rather than material

The Response to Industrialism

values. In *The Education of Henry Adams* (1907) he revealed the dilemma that the sensitive individual experienced in American industrial society.

The root of the evil, argued Godkin, who founded the *Nation*, a weekly, in 1865, lay not in corruption but in the system which bred it, the alliance between industrialists and politicians which produced benefits for business in the form of tariffs, public lands, and federal subsidies. Investigations during Grant's second term revealed that businessmen no less than politicians readily entered corrupt bargains to secure a share of the booty. This alliance could be destroyed by choosing able men as public administrators, men with a sense of responsibility to the entire community, educated men who were not involved in the pressures of economic growth and who wished nothing from office save to use their talents for the public good. The patricians exhorted the educated class to participate more actively in public affairs and called on Congress to encourage them by reforming the civil service.

Congressmen sneered at Senator Carl Schurz's (1829–1906) civil service proposals as "snivel service reform." They did not relish an innovation that would deprive them of party patronage and financial support. Only a national event of shocking proportions persuaded them to act. In 1881 a disappointed office-seeker, a member of the "stalwart" pro-Grant faction of the Republican party, assassinated President Garfield. While the President lay slowly dying for several months, the nation daily became more aware of the way in which patronage quarrels had generated the tragedy. In 1883 Congress finally passed the nation's basic civil service law, the Pendleton Act, which provided for appointments on the basis of competitive examinations. Although it originally covered only 14,000 out of 100,000 employees, most federal civil servants eventually came under its jurisdiction.

The Shock of Change

To the patricians who read the *Nation* the American party system, with its patronage, its intense party loyalty, and its political logrolling, degraded the profession of politics. Independent to the core, called Mugwumps by their opponents, they backed candidates for principles rather than party affiliations. Normally Republican, they were repelled by the corruption of the Grant administration and its harsh policy toward the South. In 1872 they hoped to challenge Grant with a third party, the Liberal Republicans; however, they lost control of their own Cincinnati nominating convention to a group of professional politicians, and their experiment failed. In 1876 they divided evenly between the two candidates, the Republican Rutherford B. Hayes (1822–93) and the Democrat Samuel J. Tilden (1814–86), both known as men of great personal political integrity, both running on a program of honest government. But in 1884, when the Republicans nominated James G. Blaine (1830–93), who was tainted by the corruption of the Grant regime, the patricians supported the Democrat, Grover Cleveland (1837–1908). Henceforth they continued to be independents, often supporting Cleveland, sometimes fluctuating between the two parties, but never gaining a large following.

FARMERS AND THE PRICE ECONOMY

Farmers, no longer relatively self-sufficient, were bewildered by the new economic conditions. They were involved now in a worldwide economic network, the impersonal price-and-market system, which they understood only dimly. Slowly and with great difficulty they learned to cope with these new problems, to calculate costs and prices with business-like efficiency, and to join together to deal with powerful market forces.

This process of adjustment gave rise to an agrarian protest movement between the Civil War and the mid-1890's. The character of the movement varied according to the level of farm income and the particular economic circumstances in different sections of the country. The two major rural outbursts, for example, the Granger and the Populist movements, occurred in periods of depression in farm prices, the first in the early 1870's, the second in the early 1890's. These revolts were most intense in the cotton South and the western wheat states where staple crops were sold in world markets for widely fluctuating prices.

As the area of wheat production moved westward, so did farm protest. The Granger movement had centered in the older wheat area of Illinois, Wisconsin, Iowa, and Minnesota; the focal point of Populism, on the other hand, lay in the new wheat belt of the Dakotas, Nebraska, and Kansas. Here collapse of the pioneer, speculative, "boomer" economy in the late 1880's intensified discontent. The former Granger area, having shifted to a dairy and corn-hog economy, in the nineties responded coolly to Populism. So did northeastern farmers who, faced with western competition, had been forced to shift from grain to domestically consumed fruit, truck, and dairy crops; they blamed the newer, lower-cost producers of the West for their troubles.

Farmers complained that their costs were too high and their prices too low. They attributed these conditions to the greediness of those in the price-and-market system with whom they had most immediate contact: the mortgage lender, so they argued, charged arbitrarily high interest rates, the railroad high transportation rates, and the merchant high prices for machinery and equipment. These claims are difficult to substantiate. Farm costs, especially of transportation, machinery, and capital, fell between 1864 and 1896. Prices, especially of commodities sold on the world market, wheat and cotton, for example, also dropped steadily during the same period. Yet, the cost of farm purchases declined slightly more than did farm prices as a whole, thereby improving farm purchasing power to a very small degree and, as one author has stated, "indicating that something besides prices alone lay beneath the long periods of farmer distress." On the other hand, fixed costs, especially high for the mechanized wheat belt, once incurred, did not fluctuate with prices. It suffices to say that farmers, comparing their livelihood with increasing urban wealth, blamed those who sold them goods and services for the gap between the two.

These targets of attack served as the specific symbols of a network of economic forces that the farmer increasingly associated with fluid wealth, the money market, the banking and currency system, and more precisely with the "capitalists" who financed business. The capitalist produced no wealth, the farmer argued, but merely manipulated it to the disadvantage of the toiling workers who created material goods by the sweat of their brows. Low prices stemmed from a shortage of circulating currency, and the currency shortage from the selfish policies of Wall Street bankers who held the financial strings of the nation in their hands. Destroy this iron grip on the nation's economy through a banking system which the federal government, the "people" rather than the "interests," would control. In this way farmers explained the impact of the impersonal revolutionary forces of industrial capitalism in terms of the personal greed of the capitalists themselves.

A sustained effort to build an effective farm organization dominated the agrarian protest movement. The Patrons of Husbandry, or Grange, the first such attempt of nationwide scope, originated in 1867 when Oliver H. Kelley (1826–1913) set out to improve rural social life. Kelley argued that the central problem for farmers lay in their isolated and drab existence. But a concern for costs and prices, he soon discovered, enrolled far more farm members than did social gatherings. Although the Grange retained many of its social trappings (a secret ritual patterned after the Masonic Order, for example), it soon placed primary stress on co-operative purchasing, marketing, and manufacturing organizations. Around these activities, farmers of the Upper Mississippi Valley flocked into the Grange during the first five years of the 1870's.

Co-operative enterprise constituted the persistent and ultimately the most successful feature of the farm movement. Yet in Granger days it invariably failed. Farmers often expanded their co-operative businesses beyond their capacity to keep them solvent; they had difficulty in finding experienced managers to operate their firms. Moreover, local merchants and middlemen, hostile to this new competitor, often had sufficient resources to outlast and destroy the farmer-owned enterprise. The Grange declined in the 1870's, but newer farm organizations known as Farmers' Alliances continued to promote co-operatives in the eighties and nineties. Although many of these also failed, some remained to form the nucleus of a third, early twentieth-century drive to organize farm co-operatives, a movement that grew steadily from that time forward.

In both the Granger and the Populist periods co-operative enterprise soon gave way to partisan political action, which to farmers seemed a more direct and immediate method of solving their problems. On the other hand, leaders of existing political parties, and erstwhile leaders anxious to acquire a party following, stimulated the movement to channel rural protest into partisan politics. Although shunning political action, the Grange inadvertently stimulated it; the organization did not officially engage in politics, but its members did. In some states the "Granger movement," a term which easterners popularized to connote western irresponsibility, worked through existing parties, and in others, such as Illinois and Iowa, it established new parties. The state "Granger laws" to regulate railroad rates and services, the movement's most significant accomplishment, were often rudimentary, rarely permanent. Greater immediate significance lay in the Granger cases, in which in 1877 the United States Supreme Court upheld the power of a state legislature to regulate railroads within its borders. The Greenback party of the late seventies and early eighties, though strongest in labor circles, also appealed for farm votes on the strength of a proposal to raise farm prices by currency inflation. But as prices and income improved in the early eighties, the Greenbackers, after winning fifteen congressional seats in 1878, quickly disappeared.

Far more comprehensive and far-reaching agrarian political action came in the early 1890's with the Populist party. Formed to participate in the election of 1890, this party flourished primarily in the farm belt of the South and the western Middle West. In 1892 the Populists nominated James B. Weaver as their candidate for President. They advocated such economic reforms as federal ownership and control of railroads and telegraph lines, nationalization of banks, currency inflation through silver coinage, and cancellation of unused railroad land grants. In 1892 they polled only 8 per cent of the national popular vote, but they showed surprising strength in the agrarian states south of the Ohio and west of the Mississippi. Although in 1894 the Populist party increased its support, by 1896 the Democrats had captured its major strength. Their influence now insignificant, the Populists struggled on until 1908.

The episodic character of the agrarian movement in the nineteenth century, its periodic outbursts, its constant shifting from economic organization to partisan political action, revealed weakness rather than strength. The revulsion from the new price-and-market system, the tendency to blame individuals for deep-seated changes in the structure of the economy, came less from a well-conceived response than from not knowing exactly how their problems might be solved. Yet within these fitful expressions of shock lay the seed of the more effective farm movement of the future—the formation of economic power that would enable the farmer to cope with the new forces. Only through bitter experience did the farmer learn how to shape such power, subject to his own control, to be used in his own interest.

In the late nineteenth century the leadership of agrarian agitation came frequently from the merchant, the farm editor, or the politician, those whose interest in farmers was secondary but who took the initiative in reform. Western and midwestern merchants spearheaded the Granger movement to regulate railroads; Chicago commodity dealers led the drive to regulate grain elevators. Western silver-mine owners, many of them multimillionaires, helped to divert the Populist movement into the free-silver issue and thereby into the Democratic party. Between 1894 and 1896 a few Populist leaders, especially agricultural editors, fought to preserve a third party that would support a broad reform program, but politicians who wished to emphasize free silver won out. These events revealed the degree to which agrarian reform was subject to manipulation by a variety of influences. Only when the farmer in the twentieth century forged his co-operative commodity organizations did he develop the independent economic power, under his own control, that enabled him to cope effectively with the price-and-market system.

WORKERS FACE THE WAGE SYSTEM

In adjusting to the new economic system workingmen experienced as many difficulties as did farmers. The new emphasis on specialization produced a profound change in the lives of artisans, stripping them of their roles of manager and salesman and reducing them to the sole task of selling their labor to others. Shocked by these innovations as deeply as farmers had been, organized workingmen for several decades adopted programs through which they hoped to destroy or to escape from the wage system and to re-establish their old position as owners of enterprise. Only gradually did they become reconciled to their new condition and concentrate on working out their lives within it. 1866-1872

Two national organizations, the National Labor Union and the Knights of Labor, dominated the movement of workingmen from the Civil War to the late 1880's. A Pennsylvania iron molder, William H. Sylvis (1828–69), guided the National Labor Union. As a young man, Sylvis had been an energetic organizer for the Iron Molders Union; but after several expensive and futile strikes by the iron molders, he had become discouraged and hostile toward trade unions. At best they were defensive, he argued, perhaps useful in preventing working conditions from deteriorating, but of no value for improving them. The real problem, he came to believe, lay in the wage system then displacing the artisan. Businessmen devised this new capitalist organization of production merely to drive independent craftsmen out of existence; it could easily be abolished by forcing employers to refrain from their selfish and evil ways.

Under Sylvis' leadership the National Labor Union during its six-year existence from 1866 until 1872 refrained from action that might render the wage system more permanent and instead advanced proposals by which wage earners could become entrepreneurs. The public lands, the Union argued, should be granted no longer to business corporations but should be reserved for settlers, perhaps workingmen seeking a new start in the West. Far more seriously considered was a proposal to supplant the wage system with co-operative production, in which workers would pool their resources, supply their own labor, and manage the factories themselves. "By cooperation," declared Sylvis, "we will become a nation of employers—the employers of our own labor. The wealth of the land will pass into the hands of those who produce it."

The Response to Industrialism

Co-operatives that the iron molders themselves established in the late 1860's frequently collapsed because of insufficient capitalization, inexperienced managers, and limited productive capacity. Small wonder that a group of workingmen experienced difficulty in keeping pace with an iron and steel industry undergoing tremendous technological change. Sylvis and the Union, however, blamed their failures primarily on the reluctance of bankers to extend them loans. Generalizing from this experience, they attributed the entire working-class problem to the money and currency system that bankers and capitalists, conspiring to enslave the workingman, manipulated in their own interest. Inspiration for such a view came from the writings of Edward Kellogg, whose book, *A New Monetary System*, was republished in 1861. Kellogg criticized private bankers and described a currency and banking system that the federal government alone would operate, lending funds and establishing interest rates, not for "private profit," but for the "general welfare." Under such a system, argued Sylvis, workingmen could obtain capital to establish co-operative production.

Stressing broad reforms obtainable only through national organization rather than trade-union action, the National Labor Union logically drifted toward independent politics. Yet this tendency only created a deep split within its ranks. Since political action required for success a far broader voting public than workingmen could muster, Sylvis invited other reformers to join with the Union. He brought socialist leaders into the movement and in 1868 insisted that Elizabeth Cady Stanton, a leading suffragette, be seated at the Union's convention. Many working-class leaders were hostile toward these innovations. A number of trade unions, more inclined to stress the eight-hour movement, at that time led by Boston machinist Ira Steward, had joined the National Labor Union in its early years. Fearing the Union's trend toward general reform rather

34

than purely working-class objectives, the trade unions left the national organization. Upon Sylvis' death in 1869, the Union's one cohesive force disappeared; rapidly disintegrating, it uttered its last gasp in the election of 1872 as the Labor Reform party.

The desire to escape from the wage system rather than to work within it as a job- and wage-conscious group continued to be manifest in a far more extensive organization, the Knights of Labor. The Knights was formed in 1869 by a Philadelphia garment cutter, Uriah Stephens (1821–82), who criticized the narrow objectives of trade unions: "It was only because the trade union failed to recognize the rights of man and looked only to the rights of the tradesman—i.e., the wage earner—that the Knights of Labor became a possibility." Stephens, who had studied for the Baptist ministry, was a religious humanitarian. Craft unions were divisive, he argued, and far less desirable than an organization bringing together all who "gained their bread by the sweat of their brow." Stephens brought to the Knights a semireligious ritual and a "vow," a form of organization quite similar to that used by the Patrons of Husbandry. A strictly secret organization in order to combat the blacklist and other employer anti-workingmen tactics, the Knights of Labor grew slowly during the depression of 1873–79. In contrast, the number of national "open" (non-secret) trade unions declined from thirty to nine in the same period. In 1878 the Knights organized on a nationwide basis. Largely because of the opposition of the Catholic church, the Knights abandoned secrecy in 1881. In 1879 Stephens was succeeded as Grand Master Workman by Terence V. Powderly (1849–1924), who led the organization through the major years of its life.

Powderly, an Irish machinist who had been mayor of Scranton, Pennsylvania, added a new twist to the reform analysis of working-class problems. The wage system, he argued, not only would de-

The Response to Industrialism

stroy the independent artisan but would create permanent economic classes and eventually social and economic chaos. "From its very nature," he wrote, "the wage system has caused employer and employed to regard each other with suspicion; it has not made the interest of employer and employed identical." Fearing class conflict, Powderly emphasized the solidarity of society. His vision of a purely classless social order persuaded him to disapprove of strikes and to encourage arbitration of all labor disputes. He boasted that as head of the Knights he never called a strike. Officially the Knights adopted the same view in its platform: "To persuade employers to agree to arbitrate all differences which may arise between them and their employees, in order that the bonds of sympathy between them may be strengthened, and that strikes may be rendered unnecessary."

Membership in the Knights of Labor skyrocketed in the mid-1880's, climbing some 700 per cent between 1885 and 1886; it then declined with almost equal rapidity. The Knights became particularly attractive to workingmen when in 1885 shopworkers on southwestern railroads won a strike against Jay Gould, one of the most notorious railroad capitalists in the country. Although victory came from the fact that Gould could not then afford the embarrassment of a contest, American workers attributed it to the power of the Knights; in one year its membership shot up from 104,000 to 702,000. A host of unplanned, reckless, and unsuccessful strikes ensued; Gould himself shattered the illusion when he precipitated one on his road and completely destroyed the union. As the Knights' membership subsequently declined, the organization increasingly assumed a rural character.

Behind this decline in strength lay rank-and-file disillusionment with the Knights' leaders. The organization had attracted workers who sought to form trade unions and to use strikes to achieve im-

36

mediate gains; but they quickly learned that the Knights' officials were hostile to this approach. In 1884 the few national trade unions then in existence laid plans for a nationwide drive for the eight-hour day to take place on May 1, 1886; this Powderly opposed as inopportune. In the fall of 1886 Powderly ordered striking Chicago meatworkers either to resume employment or lose their charters. The crowning blow came when Powderly resisted a move in the Knights' convention to express sympathy for the men accused in the Chicago Haymarket "riot" of May 4, 1886. Under such circumstances the Knights quickly lost prestige in the eyes of wage earners. Its rapid demise paved the way for a job-and-wage-oriented trade-union movement, which would concentrate on creating economic power to advance the condition of workers within the wage system.

THE FEAR OF SOCIAL CONFLICT

The discontent of workers and farmers intensified a growing social cleavage in the United States in the last third of the nineteenth century. The gulf between rich and poor, who did not share equally in the nation's growing wealth, rapidly widened. On the one hand, the wealthy spent their fortunes arrogantly in "conspicuous consumption." On the other, the urban masses lived in poverty, in slums "across the tracks." Farmers were no longer looked upon as respected yeomen. They were seen as "hicks" and "hayseeds" whose occupation seemed never to promise an urban standard of living. Immigration intensified this gulf, adding to the ranks of the urban poor and sharpening the contrast between the native American middle class and the foreign urban workingman.

The stark reality of social conflict deeply stunned Americans who had cherished the view that class divisions did not exist in their country. Historian James Ford Rhodes, who had lived during the depression of the 1870's, wrote in 1919 of the railway strikes of

The Response to Industrialism

1877: ". . . We had hugged the delusion that such social uprisings belonged to Europe and had no reason of being in a free republic where there was plenty of room and an equal chance for all." In 1885 Josiah Strong, a startled Congregational clergyman, expressed this sense of shock most vividly in a popular book, *Our Country:* fearfully he described the danger of class strife, which, he argued, immigration increased, and predicted dire social revolt. Writing a few years later, Vida D. Scudder lamented, "Cleavage of classes, cleavage of race, cleavage of faiths! an inextricable confusion. And the voice of democracy, crying aloud in our streets: 'Out of all this achieve brotherhood! achieve the race to be.'" The sharp contrast between the realities of social tension and inherited ideals of a classless society gave rise to an unusual variety of ideological reactions in the eighties and nineties. These revealed that the sense of shock prompted the public to cast social conflict from its mind or to seek solutions which would miraculously destroy it; only slowly did Americans seek to understand and to come to terms effectively with their new experience.

Many were prone to reduce complex economic and social problems to matters of private and public morality. Convinced that material success stemmed as much from moral virtue as from luck, they equally insisted that poverty arose from immorality, from a fundamental and perhaps inherent defect in character. Corrupt urban government they attributed, not to the difficulties of shaping an effective community amid such rapid change, but to the evil machinations of venal politicians who could not acquire wealth through honest business. Such leaders exhorted the poor to be honest, thrifty, and sober. They participated in sporadic campaigns for "clean government." Their efforts invariably failed because they did not—perhaps could not—meet the major problems of social adjustment and community organization. The few urban reform

38

administrations that emerged in the late nineteenth century maintained no roots among the mass of urban voters; either the electorate soon drove them from office or they came to terms with existing political organizations and thereby lost favor with reformers.

Economic views popular late in the century served to minimize the problems of social conflict and to create the notion that the personal misery caused by economic change was inconsequential compared with its benefits. One such notion, Social Darwinism, stemmed from Darwin's theory that evolution had proceeded through a process of natural selection, a struggle for existence in which the less fit perished and the more capable survived. Herbert Spencer (1820–1903), an Englishman, formulated, and John Fiske (1842–1901) popularized in the United States, a theory as to the way in which this process worked for human society, the theory of free economic competition. Success came to those who were able to survive the rigors of struggle, and the poor were poor simply because they were the less fit. Poverty was a necessary evil, and one should not try to abolish it lest he interfere with nature's laws and restrict the success of the more able. The public could safely ignore slums, long hours of work, and low living standards as sacrifices which society should accept for its own larger and more permanent good, though, many argued, the poor provided an excellent opportunity for the rich to practice Christian charity by alleviating suffering.

The view most popular among economic thinkers of the time and known as classical economics denied that a conflict existed between private and public interest. Private competition among individuals, in which each man sought his own self-interest, would automatically produce the greatest social good, according to the theory. Since no public interest existed above and beyond the sum of private interests, for the public to show concern for social conflict would

The Response to Industrialism

violate this "fundamental law of nature." Labor-management relationships should be the province solely of employers and their individual employees; urban civic problems required no special attention over and above what each individual gave to his private affairs.
To deny that in such matters a public interest existed ignored the
broader implications of the impact of industrialism and drew an
ideological curtain around private economic behavior. Only slowly
did Americans recognize that private actions involved grave public
consequences.

The fact of social disorder, however, could not be argued out of
existence; until the twentieth century the characteristic reaction to
such facts was forcibly to suppress them. A prominent businessman
tersely summed up this view when he recommended armed force to
put down a strike: "Give the workingmen and strikers gun bullet
food for a few days and you will observe how they take that sort of
bread." State and federal troops quelled numerous strikes, among
them the 1877 railroad upheavals in the Northeast, the Pullman
affair in Chicago in 1894, and innumerable disturbances among
both eastern and western miners. The Haymarket incident in Chicago was the most spectacular effort to banish industrial problems
by force. By the spring of 1886, having faced for several years a
barrage of inflammatory anarchist literature, Chicago citizens were
tense with fear. During an anarchist-led meeting a bomb exploded,
killing one policeman and fatally wounding others. Horror-struck,
the community demanded that anarchist leaders should be hanged,
even though no one could be found who actually threw the bomb.
With these hangings accomplished, the city heaved a sigh of relief,
confident that the law had suppressed the monster in its midst.
Barely a handful of Chicago citizens set forth to examine the root of
industrial unrest in their city. Yet, after the Haymarket incident,
anarchist agitation actually increased.

The Shock of Change

The impending social crisis inspired Henry George (1839–97) to probe for the cause of extensive poverty in the midst of material progress. In *Progress and Poverty* (1879) he argued that the problem lay in the natural increase in land values accompanying economic development which permitted wealth to come to the hands of those fortunate enough to own land. Since it arose from social evolution rather than from personal ability, this "unearned increment," George argued, should be made to revert to society by means of taxation. Such a tax on land would in one blow strike at the root of monopoly, increase economic opportunity, and permit other taxes to be abandoned; it would be the Single Tax. *Progress and Poverty*, widely read in the late 1880's and early 1890's, attracted considerable popularity abroad where George lectured. In America his movement served less to provide specific solutions than as a vehicle to crystallize a vague discontent.

Popular utopian novels revealed even more clearly the hope of Americans to find an easy solution to industrial problems. Of some sixty-eight such books appearing between 1865 and 1915, thirty-five were published in the seven years of unrest between 1888 and 1895. The most widely read, Edward Bellamy's (1850–98) *Looking Backward* (1888), scored an immediate success—it sold almost 400,000 copies—and inspired other hopeful authors to write in similar vein. Concerned with the impending internal crisis, each of these romantic novels argued that man was not competitive and greedy but was essentially good, innately capable of living in peace with his fellow man. Environment had thwarted these noble impulses; different circumstances would nourish them. The key lay in abundance, for when man's material wants were filled, no reason for selfishness would remain. Modern technology provided the opportunity for man to create an ideal society, free of social conflict. In *Looking Backward* a technical bureaucracy managed a completely state-owned productive system, employed a huge industrial army, and provided for the wants of each citizen, now happy in harmony with others.

Looking Backward inspired a nationwide organization of Nationalist Clubs, centers of discussion and political education, which stressed Bellamy's views, especially governmental ownership and operation of enterprise. Nationalist Clubs attracted many people of good will sensitive to the problems of industrial society yet appalled by social disorder and unwilling to approach problems by means that might increase social tension. Largely composed of middle-class professionals, the Nationalists relied on education to promote their cause; they shunned economic interest groups that chose to wield economic power to gain their ends. Bellamyites refused to join either with those Socialists who emphasized class struggle or with the organized labor movement. They co-operated with Populists early in the nineties, but when the Populist program centered on free silver, the Nationalists withdrew, disgusted at what they felt was an exhibition of self-interest. Since they conceived of society not as a collection of groups but as a mass of individuals bound together in a spiritual brotherhood, Bellamyites failed to co-operate with the very people whose increasing influence could effect social change.

Fear of internal discord gave rise to an increasingly vibrant nationalism in the nineties. The Sons of the American Revolution, organized in 1889, was only one of a dozen hereditary societies among the well-to-do who wanted to perpetuate a spirit of patriotism. Campaigns to stir up Americanism grew in intensity, reaching, for example, the public schools, which increasingly emphasized flag exercises and other professions of loyalty. A new belligerence toward foreign governments appeared in relations with Chile, Venezuela, and finally Cuba. Hostility toward immigrants played an especially vital role in this outburst of nationalism. Increasingly associating the "social problem" with immigration, Americans attributed poverty, vice, corrupt urban government, and the general disorganization of urban life to the newcomers. Feeding on the fear of social disunity, nativist movements grew up rapidly to purge the country of its divisive "foreign" elements.

THE TURMOIL OF THE NINETIES

A series of events in the 1890's sharpened and intensified reactions to industrialism and heightened the shock of rapid change. The Haymarket affair of 1886 was only the initial episode in a decade of incidents. In 1892 a strike at the Carnegie-owned Homestead, Pennsylvania, steel plant brought a bloody clash between strikers and Pinkerton detectives. With the deep depression of 1893 this tension erupted into nationwide turmoil. In 1894 in the Pullman strike, President Cleveland called out federal troops to suppress a bitter contest in Chicago between the American Railway Union and the roads radiating from that city. Urban workers, whom the depression hit especially hard, organized a number of spectacular marches to Washington—Jacob Coxey's (1854–1951) "army" was the most famous—to register a futile plea for public works for the unemployed. Throughout the nineties, recurrent strife gripped the coal fields of Colorado and Pennsylvania.

Events other than industrial unrest testified to the impact of the depression; it also brought fear of the foreigner to a head. The American Protective Association, the most spectacular of many anti-Catholic groups in the country, suddenly sprang to new life. Organized in the early nineties by Henry F. Bowers, the APA had reached a membership of only seventy thousand by 1893; yet during the first part of 1894 its numbers climbed to a half-million, spreading from its original centers in Michigan, Iowa, and Minne-

43

sota to the West and the East. The APA had raised traditional and oft-repeated fears of Catholic Popery in America, had allied itself with the Republican party, and had especially attacked Catholic influence in schools. Exploiting the impact of the depression, it blamed the collapse on the Catholics and warned of impending attempts by Rome to seize power. A depression-fed movement, the APA died rapidly after 1894 and was completely smothered in the free-silver agitation of the nineties. Yet the nativism which it espoused struck deep roots, though in a milder form, in the agrarian protest movement of that decade. Both Populism and the Bryan movement within the Democratic party carried ominous overtones of native, Protestant Americanism and even of anti-Semitism.

The stress of economic hardship drove a wedge between agriculture and labor. In preceding years active elements of the two groups had maintained a common effort to protect the independent entrepreneur. But as the city worker gave up his ideal of independence and became reconciled to his role as a wage earner, he ceased to have common ground with the farmer. The depression sharpened this split. Farm spokesmen had not been friendly toward the philosophy of Henry George that inspired many labor leaders; George's Single Tax, instead of reducing the tax burden as rural reformers wished, would throw it exclusively on owners of real estate. Rural leaders would not support the eight-hour day which farmers could not enjoy. As the depression wore on, farm leaders became more critical of the power of organized labor, expressing hostility to the Homestead strikers and raising a chorus of criticism of the American Railway Union in the Pullman strike, which Populist leaders themselves refused to aid. The two groups differed sharply over the tariff, the farmer demanding lower rates on manufactured goods, the urban laborer looking to the tariff as job protection. Even more significant, city workers opposed the rural plan to inflate the currency by coining silver, because it would raise prices and increase the urban cost of living. When Samuel Gompers (1850–1924), president of the American Federation of Labor, in 1896 supported William Jennings Bryan (1860–1925), the agrarian Democratic candidate for President, he received censure from many in the rank and file. High strategy and common enemies drew Gompers to Bryan, but when it came to specific actions, workers realized that farmers were as hostile to their interests as were employers.

Bitter warfare within each political party clearly revealed the turmoil of the nineties. Agrarians moved from the Populist party into the western wing of the Democratic party; in 1896 they captured the party machinery, nominated Bryan as the Democratic presidential candidate, and persuaded the convention to support the coinage of silver. A brilliant and popular orator with a magic touch, Bryan in the early nineties had served his Nebraska district in Congress, where he had become a leader of the silver bloc. His western rural audiences listened with rapt attention and responded with enthusiasm when he proclaimed: "The great cities rest upon our broad and fertile prairies. Burn down your cities and leave our farms, and your cities will spring up again as if by magic; but destroy our farms and the grass will grow in the streets of every city in the country."

A strong segment of eastern gold Democrats, bitterly hostile to silver coinage, refused to accept Bryan's candidacy, formed the National Democratic party, and nominated Senator John M. Palmer of Illinois for the presidency. The Republican party also split. When its St. Louis convention in 1896 nominated William McKinley (1843–1901) for President and went on record for the gold standard, a sizable contingent of western silver Republicans under the leadership of Henry M. Teller bolted the convention and supported Bryan. These spectacular events overshadowed the significantly large number of splinter parties that cluttered state ballots and revealed the extent of the discontent seething under the pressure of economic adversity.

The election of 1896 was one of the most tensely fought in American history. To eastern leaders, the Bryan campaign seemingly threatened to disrupt society. Behind Bryan many perceived the figure of a Democratic politician they feared even more, the former Governor John P. Altgeld (1847–1902) of Illinois. Although ineligible, because of his foreign birth, for the Democratic nomination in 1896, Altgeld remained one of the most influential men in the party and did much to add labor planks to the 1896 Democratic platform. In 1893 Altgeld had pardoned the three men who though implicated in the Haymarket affair had not been hanged, and the following year he had protested when Cleveland used federal troops in the Pullman strike. Both these actions outraged easterners, who henceforth looked upon the Illinois governor as almost an anarchist himself. Opposition to Bryan as well as to Altgeld rose to fever heat in the campaign; upon Bryan's defeat the eastern critics were convinced that civilization had barely been saved.

Political repercussions of the turmoil of the nineties appeared most dramatically in violent shifts in voting behavior. The election returns of 1894 and 1896 revealed "one of the greatest bloodless political realignments that this country has ever experienced." In 1894 the Republicans secured control of the House with the largest gain in a congressional election in the nation's modern history; in that year the Democrats failed to return a single member to Congress in twenty-four states. The presidential race in 1896 produced equally strong shifts in sentiment. Western states, customarily with large Republican majorities, veered to the Democrats by twenty or thirty percentage points, while eastern states, especially in the cities, swung toward the Republicans by almost as much. Such a violent shift in two directions at once was unique in American politics. The agrarian-oriented Democratic party gained in western silver-mining states, in the wheat belt, and in many rural sections even of the East; it lost heavily in the cities and in other areas of large industrial employment such as the upper peninsula of Michigan. The Republican gains of 1894, which continued over into 1896, were largely urban. The precise nature of this new strength is not yet clear, but it appears to have been composed largely of workers and immigrants who blamed the Democrats for the depression and who were suspicious of the economic interests and the nativist tinges of the farmers.

The fitful attempts to grapple with rapid change by desperately reaffirming the old familiar ways of life stemmed from the shock of industrialization. The turmoil of the last few years of the eighties and the early nineties, however, brought home these problems in such a way that they could not be ignored. Nor could they be dealt with only by logical theories or glorious hopes. The early years of the twentieth century, the Progressive period in American history, witnessed a stage in the adjustment to industrialism far different from that of the late nineteenth century. Concerned citizens gave increasing attention to coping concretely with the new conditions. Patrician reformers dropped their reliance on negative government and asserted the need for positive action to give direction and order to social change; labor and agriculture, accepting their new economic condition, strove to construct the power to advance their welfare within society; those concerned with social tension examined more closely its causes and proposed more concrete and immediate solutions. Twentieth-century Americans slowly learned how to live with a new industrial system that they could not and did not choose to destroy.

III. Organize or Perish

Businessmen, farmers, and workers individually could not cope with the impersonal price-and-market network, but they soon discovered that as organized groups they could wield considerable power. Individual economic enterprise, therefore, gave way to collective effort. Producers joined to control the conditions under which they sold their commodities; distributors combined to wield influence over marketing and transportation; workingmen formed trade unions to bargain with management over wages, hours, and working conditions; farmers and industrial consumers joined to reduce purchasing costs. Only urban consumers failed to unite. This organizational revolution gathered momentum after the mid-nineties and continued with increasing force in the first half of the twentieth century. It revealed the degree to which industrialism had shifted the context of economic decisions from personal relationships among individuals to a struggle for power among well-organized groups.

CORPORATE BUSINESS POWER

The business community took the initiative in the organizational revolution. Business commanded enormous resources of capital,

48

technical and managerial skills, and public influence; the groups which it formed became the most powerful in the country. The corporation itself departed sharply from individual enterprise by combining the resources of a great number of people in a joint endeavor. Corporations possessed enormous potentialities for growth; as industrialization proceeded so did their size and scope, their resources and their power. The essence of technology lay in precise and orderly manipulation of the factors of production. Industrial leaders tried to control an ever larger number of elements bearing on the business undertaking—prices, markets, sources of raw materials, labor's willingness to work, legal conditions, and public opinion. The requirements of technology pushed ever wider the factors that the entrepreneur wished to bring under his influence; the power inherent in the corporation enabled him to exercise that control.

Toward the end of the nineteenth century American economic conditions encouraged a rapid growth in corporate size. Mass markets and mass production had ushered in an era of intense competition. But competition, constantly tending to push production beyond the capacity of markets, gave rise to uneasiness in the minds of businessmen; by driving prices downward it threatened both immediate profits and long-range industrial stability. Entrepreneurs looked for methods of manipulating market forces to control competition. They experimented with a variety of techniques before discovering the most effective one.

In the 1870's the pool, a gentlemen's agreement unenforceable at law, was widely used to establish minimum prices, to control production, and to divide markets. Such agreements, however, placed a severe strain upon the integrity of gentlemen; many succumbed to the temptation to cut their own prices. These "loose combinations" arose most frequently in periods of market crisis but were evaded as soon as times looked better and then restored when a price collapse recurred. The Standard Oil Company pioneered in a tighter and more effective form of business co-operation—the trust. Stockholders of a number of competing companies gave their voting stock to a central group of trustees in return for trust certificates bearing the right to receive interest payments but not to vote. A central body, therefore, could determine common price and market policies for the entire group. The trust ran afoul both the common law and state statutes and was soon abandoned. It was superseded by the holding company, a single firm which held a controlling share of the securities of a number of subordinate firms. Encouraged by a general incorporation act for such firms passed by the New Jersey legislature in 1889, the holding company became an extremely popular form of organization, and New Jersey, in turn, became the official home of a considerable portion of the nation's industrial enterprise.

The movement to form these "tight combinations" proceeded rapidly during the prosperity years between 1897 and 1903, the first great age of business mergers in industrial America. Two factors explain the timing of these consolidations: the desire to improve market power during the boom and the phenomenal success of a number of tight combinations, such as Standard Oil and the American Tobacco Company, in weathering the financial storms of 1893–96. From 1897 to 1903 the number of combinations rose from 12 to 305, with an increase in aggregate capital from under $1 billion to nearly $7 billion. By 1904 these firms controlled nearly two-fifths of the capital in manufacturing in the United States. In 1901 appeared the largest of all, the United States Steel Company, capitalized at $1.4 billion. This mammoth merger brought into one organization some 158 corporations, including the two largest integrated steel companies in the country.

Management in areas other than industry also sought to limit competition. Even before the age of industrial mergers, the railroads had tried to establish intercompany co-operation after having experienced a period of competitive and excessive construction and subsequent bitter rivalry for business. Working agreements and outright mergers grew out of the periodic financial crises, especially that of 1893, which so deeply involved railroads. The golden era of railroad consolidation came between 1893 and 1900; by the latter year 95 per cent of the nation's railroad mileage lay in six large systems, controlled by the capitalists who financed the consolidations. Where actual merger proved to be impossible, entrepreneurs experimented with "traffic associations," pools to establish rates and divide traffic so as to eliminate pressure for "cutthroat competition." The Omaha Pool among roads operating between Chicago and Omaha was the most successful. Not until Congress perfected the regulatory machinery of the Interstate Commerce Commission, however, did rates fully become stabilized; governmental action brought order to the railroads where private competition had not.

Industrial and railroad consolidations depended on the financial resources of investment houses in the Northeast and abroad. Whether financiers or business promoters engineered most mergers is not yet fully clear. Evidence indicates that financiers did not take the initiative to the extent formerly believed. The success of mergers depended even more on the underlying desire of management to escape the insecurities of competition. Once having granted financial aid, however, the investment bankers demanded considerable control of the new firms; a large share of the mergers fell into the hands of such banking houses as J. P. Morgan and Company or Kuhn, Loeb and Company, ushering in a period in American history known as "finance capitalism." Executives in the combinations frequently became the agents of financiers, and subsequent economic policies, dictated by the bankers' interest in a safe investment, became more conservative. At the same time, the investment bankers, who frequently were more sensitive to public opinion than were business managers in the plant, often forced their executives to come to terms with public sentiment. Thus, in 1900 and 1902 J. P. Morgan (1836–1913) persuaded Pennsylvania coal operators to settle disputes with striking miners in order to prevent political repercussions potentially detrimental to the business community.

It should not be thought that the vision of more efficient production stimulated the merger movement. To be sure, elements such as more efficient marketing were involved; but far more important was the desire of entrepreneurs to escape the rigors of competition, to form market power to intervene in impersonal economic conditions before which, as individuals, they had formerly stood helpless. Moreover, these efforts succeeded. For the first time in the history of the industry, for example, the United States Steel Corporation stabilized the price of steel rails; although prior to the merger rail prices had fluctuated from year to year, they now remained at a constant level of $28 a ton. Through the famous "Gary dinners," at which Elbert H. Gary of United States Steel brought executives together, market conditions were stabilized over an even wider area of the industry.

The business corporation sought to control not only market forces but also a wider range of factors impinging upon industrial production. Some of these could be incorporated outright into a single firm. Inventors and lawyers, for example, became hired employees of corporations, losing their status as independent enterprisers. Industrial sales departments could undertake jobbing and wholesaling. Yet other factors could not be manipulated simply by bringing them directly into the orbit of the firm's management. Labor, for example, resisted such direction; entrepreneurs, in turn, feared organized labor because it constituted a factor in industrial production not easily manipulated. Arguing that collective bargaining was illegal and un-American, business demanded that wages and working conditions be determined by bargaining between the individual worker and the corporation; management could control individual bargaining far more easily than it could influence collective bargaining. Business leaders assumed an increasingly aggressive role in the struggle against organized labor. Through a number of nationwide organizations, notably the National Association of Manufacturers, business fought both collective bargaining and union recognition in local communities, in political parties, and in the halls of Congress.

To avoid the antibusiness sentiment that might lead to detrimental legislation, business also became increasingly sensitive to public opinion. When laws to regulate business first appeared, industrial leaders, for example, William H. Vanderbilt of the New York Central Railroad, had assumed a "public-be-damned" attitude, blurting out that the public had no legitimate interest in what seemed to them essentially private affairs. Once convinced, however, that the threat of regulatory legislation was serious, business became more concerned with practical techniques to prevent such adverse results. Industrial leaders became more cautious in expressing their attitudes toward the public; they now argued that the public did have a legitimate interest in the conduct of private business, though they circumscribed the area of such interest as closely as they deemed politically practical. To prevent regulatory laws, they participated more actively in politics as candidates for office, as party officials, and in providing party financial support. Forced to accept regulatory commissions, they sought to influence them in their own interest, accepting such bodies as buffers between business and the public. A commission was worth the sacrifice if it would allay antibusiness feeling and if it could be rendered harmless by a judicious choice of personnel. Becoming increasingly concerned with the need to influence public opinion directly, business leaders hired public relations counsels. The first of importance, Ivy Lee (1877–1934), tried to counteract the public's unfavorable attitude toward the Rockefellers, which had reached new heights in 1913–14 during the bitter miners' strike against the Rockefeller-owned Colorado Fuel and Iron Company.

DISTRIBUTORS' ORGANIZATIONS

While many business organizations arose from problems of industrial production, others stemmed from drastic modifications in commercial practices created by the transportation and communications revolution. Merchants became alarmed at the attempts of manufacturers to supplant professional distributors or to bring them under close control. To meet this threat in the 1890's, wholesalers and retailers among druggists, grocers, furniture dealers, hardware merchants, and farm-equipment distributors formed state and national organizations. To promote sales efficiency, the new combinations often reduced their traveling sales force by 20 to 50 per cent; in response, traveling salesmen organized vigorously to oppose the merger movement. These organizations did not distinguish between practices which might be considered restraints of trade, such as rebates to entice distributors not to handle a competitor's commodity, and efficiencies in marketing, such as mail-order houses. They bitterly fought the extension of rural free delivery and parcel post, which, they argued, were monopolistic proposals by manufacturers, department stores, and mail-order firms to ruin "legitimate trade." They attempted to boycott both fellow distributors who traded with these "monopolies" and the "monopolies" themselves, thereby opening their own groups to the charge of seeking to restrain trade.

Manufacturers and merchants combined to combat an even more

widespread menace, an unpopular pattern of railroad rates. The background for railroad regulation lay, not simply in the railroads' desire for maximum rates and maximum profits, but in the changing economic relationships that the new transportation created. In forging a more national economy the roads had modified drastically the flow of goods and commerce within the country; rate patterns which they established affected the rise or decline of commercial centers. Rates from the interior to the Atlantic Coast, for example, might favor New York over Baltimore or in the opposite direction might encourage the transfer of wholesaling activities from seaboard centers to inland points. New rate policies, moreover, destroyed a pattern of many small hubs from which commercial activities radiated, and they forged a system of fewer, though larger, commercial centers such as New York, Philadelphia, Chicago, and St. Louis. These newer centers became the major competitive points in the industrial economy, a fact that tended to reduce shipping costs between them and in turn persuaded industry to concentrate there. Enjoying no such reductions, shippers at intermediate points, with no competitive transportation, complained that they were forced unfairly to pay a per-ton-mile rate higher than that charged to shippers at terminal points. Smaller communities in particular blamed their decline or lack of relative growth on railroad policies tending to centralize economic functions.

The burst of organized activity around the turn of the century to control railroad rates stemmed also from a gradual rise in rates and reduction in services. Prior to 1899 transportation costs had declined steadily, and to attract business each road had extended its services. But beginning in 1899, in response to the general rise in prices in the economy, railroads advanced their rates. Shippers, therefore, complained not simply of discrimination in rates but also of their increase. Eastern farmers, subject to western competition, and merchants and industrial producers who opposed charges more favorable to their competitors complained of rate discrimination. But western and southern farm-commodity groups were especially concerned with the level of rates to northeastern markets.

In the late nineties and the early twentieth century, shippers organized to secure legislation to supervise railroads and to influence subsequent regulatory machinery. Local chambers of commerce, trade associations, and manufacturing bodies concentrated on the cost of shipping; if they were not organized specifically for that purpose, special traffic departments constituted the group's most important function. National commercial associations such as the National Board of Trade, the National Business League, and the United States Chamber of Commerce co-ordinated local movements into a nationwide protest. Although farm-commodity organizations helped to arouse farmers and thereby to provide needed support among voters, merchants and industrial producers assumed the burden of agitation.

After the Supreme Court had ruled in the Wabash case of 1886 that states could not regulate interstate commerce in the absence of federal law, Congress in the following year established the Interstate Commerce Commission with power to investigate rate complaints and to end discrimination. But in the Maximum Freight Rate case (1897) the Court destroyed the Commission's effectiveness; it declared that although the ICC could set aside any existing rate as unfair, it did not have power to establish a fair rate in its place. Shippers immediately bombarded Congress with letters and petitions to secure a more effective statute and formed the Interstate Commerce Law Convention to lobby toward such an end. Prodded by the popular and politically astute President Theodore Roosevelt (1858–1919), Congress in 1906 passed the Hepburn Act, which reinvigorated the Commission by granting it power to establish new, legal rates when it declared older ones void. In 1910, in the Mann-Elkins Act, shippers obtained for the Commission two new important powers: to set aside a rate increase temporarily, upon complaint, until the Commission had investigated to establish its fairness and to initiate proceedings in a rate case without a shipper's formal request for action. Congress increased the Commission's effectiveness even further in 1913. During the closing days of the Taft administration it granted the ICC power to establish the physical value of railroad property as a base from which to calculate fair earnings; with this standard the Commission could then determine fair rates.

Shippers eagerly utilized this machinery. Complaints appeared before the Commission in great number; most of these were decided in the shippers' favor. Prior to World War I, in fact, the shippers defeated almost every effort to raise rates. By 1916, therefore, they had come to look upon the Interstate Commerce Commission as their protector against the railroads; men favorable to their point of view often had been appointed to its ranks. Only when the federal government seized and operated the roads during World War I and suspended the powers of the ICC did the roads obtain significant rate advances. After the war, shippers demanded that the roads be returned to their owners and that the Commission's powers be restored.

To modify unfavorable transportation conditions, shippers also hoped to improve inland waterway commerce. The decline in river transport they blamed on monopolistic railroad practices; its revival could force the roads to modify their rates. A multitude of commercial organizations painted in glowing terms the future development of their communities if local streams could be made navigable. They demanded that federal appropriations for river improvement, a program first established in 1824, be expanded to finance new projects. Regional organizations, composed almost exclusively of merchants and manufacturers, arose to boost larger proposals. Two dwarfed all others: the Lakes-to-the-Gulf Deep Waterway, a channel sufficient for ocean-going vessels from Chicago to the mouth of the Mississippi via the Illinois River; and the Atlantic Coastal Deep Waterway, to follow the coast from Boston to Texas, via canals across Cape Cod and Florida.

Congress hesitated to approve such costly projects. The Rivers and Harbors Committee of the House, which had jurisdiction over river-development plans, reflected the interests of eastern and western coastal ports and Great Lakes shippers. It was unfriendly toward the commercial aspirations of towns on the rivers of the interior part of the country. To muster public sentiment for their projects, the inland-waterway promoters organized the National Rivers and Harbors Congress, which after 1905 met annually. Composed of commercial bodies, and studded with congressional leaders as honorary officials, this organization by 1910 secured a more friendly congressional committee. Their movement received a boost from President Roosevelt in 1907 when he appointed an Inland Waterways Commission to investigate the possibilities of combining river transportation development with a multiple-purpose inland-waterway program involving waterpower, flood control, and reclamation. Having aroused the country, the shippers obtained a few of their most promising projects; the Mississippi and Atlantic coastal waterways were begun, though more limited in scope than when first proposed, and after several decades of construction were finally completed.

THE FARM CO-OPERATIVE MOVEMENT

The new farm organization after the mid-nineties became increasingly similar in purpose to industrial and distributors' groups.

Organize or Perish

Far more concerned with the specific business problems of farmers than Grangers and Populists had been, farmers now formed commodity organizations that dealt with the economic problems facing producers of particular crops. To tackle railroad transportation conditions, for example, Iowa stockmen in 1904 formed the Corn Belt Meat Producers Association. The twentieth-century farm movement, rising from an unprecedented period of farm prosperity rather than from depression, concentrated, not on sweeping social changes that would arrest economic innovations, but on forming the organized power that would enable farmers to improve their position piecemeal within the new economic system. Far less spectacular though more profound in its consequences than former farm movements had been, the new trend in agricultural organization reflected the adjustment of farmers to a business society.

The most characteristic form of organization was the producers' co-operative, a farmer-owned processing or distributing enterprise specializing in particular commodities. Co-operative purchasing agencies, though subordinate to these ventures, frequently accompanied them. Prominent farmers, editors of farm journals, and officials of farm organizations took the initiative in forming co-operative grain elevators, livestock shipping associations, and cotton warehouses. The co-operative differed from the ordinary corporation in two important respects. Each individual in the enterprise cast only one vote; his voice did not depend upon the amount of stock he owned. Moreover, the co-operative did not make profits. Its surpluses were considered as undercharges when buying from farmers or as overcharges when selling to them. They were returned to customers as patronage dividends in proportion to the amount of business the customer had carried on with the co-operative. Hiring expert general managers to conduct their affairs, co-operatives became as efficient as business corporations. They secured state laws to protect legally their form of organization, finally persuaded the state agricultural colleges to take up co-operative and marketing problems, and in 1912 secured in the Department of Agriculture a co-operative fact-finding agency, the Bureau of Markets.

The first co-operatives in the United States came in the dairy industry, where more efficient community butter and cheese plants replaced home production. Owned by small groups of farmers, these creameries took up co-operative marketing, supervising butter and cheese sales in distant areas. Many such creameries, in turn, co-ordinated their marketing in regional organizations. The Minnesota Cooperative Creameries Association, for example, formed in 1911, sold the produce of some 130 member co-operatives and operated a commission house in New York City. By 1926 this organization of 503 member co-operatives, now known as the Land O'Lakes Creameries, had become one of the largest co-operative dairy enterprises in the world.

Co-operative organizations also gathered grain and livestock in local communities to be forwarded to terminal markets. Arising from dissatisfaction with the costs and services of marketing, these firms sought to reduce expenses by displacing the middleman. Both Grangers and Alliancemen had experimented unsuccessfully with co-operative elevators; but revived in the late nineties, the movement grew and expanded without interruption. By 1904 some one hundred co-operative, farmer-owned elevators flourished in the wheat and corn belts; by 1921, five thousand. Livestock shipping associations by 1916 reached the number of five hundred, a figure doubled by 1920. As with the dairy organizations, the grain and meat co-operatives reached out to encompass more of the marketing process. They sought to establish at the major market centers farmer-owned stockyards and grain elevators, which would receive produce from the local co-operatives and return to them the middle-man's usual profits as patronage dividends. But these ventures encountered opposition from commission men, who feared competition from farmer-owned enterprise. Organized in boards of trade that controlled admission to trading on the terminal markets, commission men refused to accept co-operatives as legitimate merchants and boycotted those who tried to enter the market without official sanction. Rebuffed here, the co-operatives carried their case to Congress; in 1921, in the Grain Futures Act and the Packers and Stockyards Act, they obtained laws prohibiting discrimination against farmer-owned terminal projects.

By more efficient marketing these co-operatives hoped to return to the farmer the middleman's profits. Other co-operatives tried to influence the level of market prices as well. Much as industry entered agreements to establish minimum prices, a number of rural leaders hoped that farmers could agree not to sell below a fixed price. The American Society of Equity in the early part of the twentieth century organized "holding campaigns," exhorting farmers to hold their produce from the market unless offered an established price. Such movements failed until more tightly formed "contract-type co-operatives" took them up. Members of this form of co-operative signed a contract requiring them to ship all their produce through a central organization or pay a heavy fine. The central body could then control the flow of commodities to market and could bargain with distributors and processors for higher prices. Especially adapted to the producers of fruit and vegetable crops grown in relatively compact geographical areas, the contract-type organization first became successful in the California citrus industry. The Southern California Fruit Exchange, organized in 1895, became the pattern for this type of marketing organization, which grew rapidly in the second and third decades of the twentieth century. Applied especially to truck, fruit, and dairy products, the contract-type co-operative became the device whereby agricultural producers established collective bargaining and obtained a high degree of power and control over the price-and-market system.

Commodity organizations became the source of strength for the new farm politics that stressed non-partisan, "pressure-group" activity rather than third parties. In the first decade of the twentieth century state-wide commodity organizations emerged to tackle through legislation such problems as railroad rates and services, terminal stockyard facilities, and competition with non-co-operative enterprise. They hired lobbyists and lawyers to fight their battles before state and national legislatures. They supplied the legal talent to file complaints and conduct cases before the Interstate Commerce Commission. When the co-operatives were challenged as contrary to the Sherman Antitrust Act, they secured from Congress exemptions from such prosecution both in the Clayton Act of 1914 and again in the Capper-Volstead Act of 1922. Commodity groups and especially the co-operatives constituted the basic instruments of political power among the more commercial and business-like farmers of the country.

Two general farm organizations also championed the farmers' cause in the early twentieth century: the National Farmers Union and the American Society of Equity. Yet the interests and problems of co-operatives strongly influenced the objectives of these groups, and to a large extent they devoted their activity to the expansion of co-operation. The strength of the Farmers Union lay in the tobacco, cotton, and wheat regions of the South and West. The Farmers Union sponsored co-operative organization in buying and selling; it developed state-wide merchandising facilities, owned a coal mine in Colorado and a bank in Mississippi. Disavowing partisan politics, the Union participated actively in non-partisan business politics on the state and national level. Charles Barrett, its president from 1906 to 1928, became known as one of the most powerful lobbyists in Washington. Sponsoring general legislation of economic interest to the farmer, rather than specific measures desired by particular commodity groups, the Union helped to secure the Parcels Post Act of 1910 and the Federal Farm Loan Act of 1916.

The American Society of Equity, its membership concentrated in the Wisconsin-Minnesota-Dakota region, attended more particularly to problems of the northern wheat belt. One of its principal accomplishments was to found the Equity Cooperative Exchange, a terminal grain-marketing organization in Minneapolis. Its widely publicized "wheat-holding" campaigns, though spectacular at the time, had less permanent significance. Active in politics especially in Wisconsin, the Equity backed laws to legalize and encourage farm co-operatives and to establish a state-operated binder twine plant at the Wisconsin state prison. In Wisconsin, Equity participated in the partisan politics more characteristic of earlier farm movements; it became closely associated with the La Follette group in the Republican party and supported a wide variety of economic and political reforms.

BUSINESS UNIONISM

The trend toward economic organization and business politics transformed American labor from a diffuse, general reform movement into a compact, disciplined fighting group seeking limited and concrete economic gains. Fearing the wage system, organized labor prior to the late 1880's had concentrated on political and economic measures designed to promote ownership of the means of production. But the wage system was a permanent fact, an indispensable element of mass production, and with it came a permanent wage-earning working class, concerned primarily with selling its labor at favorable prices. Accepting this innovation, new labor organizations concentrated on improving their position within the wage system instead of seeking to escape from it into ownership.

The new movement found expression in the American Federation of Labor, formed in 1886, and quite different from the earlier Knights of Labor. The AF of L's membership was confined to skilled workers, whereas the Knights had welcomed all "producers," skilled or unskilled; it was organized on the basis of trades instead of in the geographical assemblies that characterized the Knights. It rejected attempts to form an independent labor party, preferring to make its weight felt through non-partisan political action; and it vigorously entered into the struggle against management with all the economic weapons at its disposal, whereas the Knights had emphasized conciliation, shunning any action that would destroy the solidarity of interests in society. Yet each of these differences reflected a more basic fact, that the Federation accepted the implications of modern industrialism, the wage system, which the Knights had not.

Prior to the transportation revolution, control of the local labor supply through local unions sufficed to maintain wages and working standards; such unions arose first in the 1830's. But the new national market, making it possible for labor competition in one area of the country to drive down wages and working conditions in another, gave rise to national trade unions that could establish national working standards. A few such organizations appeared in the 1850's, but most did not survive the Civil War period and the depression of the 1870's. (An exception was the International Typographical Workers, founded in 1850, which has enjoyed a continuous existence to the present day.) The new unions, moreover, became increasingly effective. Higher dues added to the unions' financial resources, thereby enabling them more effectively to survive a prolonged strike. National organizations secured tighter control over the activities of locals to insure more co-ordinated action; the national body frequently obtained power to force the transfer of surplus funds from strong to weak locals in times of crisis and could exercise a veto power on strikes. To increase loyalty to the organization, unions devised a more effective benefit program of sickness, disability, and death payments. A growing number of national trade unions copied these techniques that were first adopted by the Cigarmakers International Union under the leadership of Samuel Gompers.

Gompers, an English immigrant, had come to America in 1863 at the age of thirteen. The following year he joined the cigarmakers union, and in little over a decade he became its dominant figure. Gompers preached widely the new approach of "business unionism." He insisted that the trade union was intensely "practical," not concerned with general theories of society or comprehensive, utopian solutions. Copying British trade unionism, Gompers emphasized the immediate economic problems of wage earners: wages, hours, accidents, and other working conditions. He would not be diverted into other fields of action, such as general reform movements or women's suffrage or temperance, but confined working-class activity solely to the economic problems of wage earners. This was "pure and simple" trade unionism. The immediate objective of the new unionism was to fashion a powerful and effective economic organization, geared to economic struggle with employers, using a full array of economic weapons—the union label, the strike, the boycott. The new unionism, far different in philosophy from the Knights, rested frankly upon the assumption that a fundamental conflict of interest existed between employer and employee and that relatively few employees could ever become employers.

The Response to Industrialism

Such a philosophy did not persuade the new trade unions to avoid politics; on the contrary, they participated actively in elections and in legislative affairs. But they held a new conception of both the end and the means of political action, new views consistent with the new orientation of their organizations. Above all, political action should serve the basic economic goals of wage earners. It should, for example, be used to secure laws to legalize trade-union tactics, to permit boycotts and picketing. But one should not participate in political action for more general reforms, which would only vitiate the trade-union movement. More effective union action, moreover, could not be achieved by partisan politics, either through one of the major parties or an independent movement; these would necessitate compromise, water down the trade-union program in favor of non-trade-union reforms, and dissipate the organization's energies in causes remote from its immediate interests. Pure and simple unionism, on the other hand, required non-partisan politics, support of those candidates in either party who would espouse the union's legislative demands. This was the business politics of business unionism.

Under Gompers' inspiration, the AF of L came into being as a federation of national trade unions. The AF of L grew slowly; by 1898 its membership had reached only 278,000. It gained some support among workers in 1890 when a Federation-sponsored drive for the eight-hour day among the carpenters succeeded; but this movement quickly declined and after 1891 was left for the individual unions to continue. The AF of L, however, shared with other economic groups the six years of general prosperity after 1898; dues to finance a vigorous organizational campaign poured into its coffers, and membership by 1904 reached 1,676,200.

This rapid growth produced increasing uneasiness about organized labor on the part of industrial leaders; in 1902 they began to come together to combat the challenge. John Kirby, Jr., of Dayton, Ohio, formed local employer associations throughout the Middle West to drive unions from their towns; manufacturers faced with boycotts in 1903 organized the Anti-Boycott Association to prosecute, under the Sherman Antitrust Act, unions engaging in such action. In 1902 President David Parry of the National Association of Manufacturers swung his organization behind the drive to turn back the tide of unionism. These efforts contributed to a decline in union membership to about 1,400,000 by 1909.

Employers sought to cripple organized labor through legal action to restrain its activities. Prevailing doctrine accepted unions as such as legal but distinguished carefully between their legal and illegal actions. Courts usually interpreted narrowly the acceptable limits of union activity; they frequently granted employers injunctions, court orders which prohibited the use of such weapons as the boycott and the "we don't patronize list." Moreover, in the Danbury Hatters case (1908) the Supreme Court upheld a damage suit against a union for engaging in a boycott, which, the Justices argued, constituted a restraint of trade under the Sherman Antitrust Act. Even more ominous to organized labor, the court in the Hatters case intimated—lower courts later repeated the view more clearly—that the mere existence of a union, if it represented all workers in the entire nation producing a given product, would be a monopoly and therefore illegal.

These events aroused the AF of L to vigorous political action designed to limit the use of the injunction and to prohibit prosecutions of labor organizations under the Sherman Act. This campaign, instituted in 1904, and increasing in intensity each congressional election, was strictly non-partisan. Yet Democrats proved to be far more friendly to labor than were Republicans. When AF of L leaders in 1906 presented a "Bill of Grievances" outlining their legislative demands to Republican leaders, including President Theodore Roosevelt, they were rebuffed; they met a similar reaction before the resolutions committee of the Republican National Convention of 1908. But the same year the Democrats incorporated into their platform planks which labor had prepared. In 1910, when the Democrats obtained control of the House, they placed men friendly to labor on the House Committee on Labor, an action which the Republicans had refused to take, and chose as the committee's chairman a former union official, William B. Wilson of Pennsylvania. As a result of these changes organized labor won its first major legislative victory in years, the creation of a Department of Labor. President Woodrow Wilson, elected in 1912, continued this recognition of labor when he appointed William B. Wilson as the first Secretary of Labor.

Labor's specific legislative program achieved only limited success. Although the Clayton Antitrust Act of 1914 reaffirmed the view that labor organizations as such were legal, it did not exempt unions from prosecution under the antitrust laws, nor did it effectively restrict the use of the injunction. Workers achieved far more significant gains when the Wilson administration constantly supported, in word and in deed, the view that organized labor and collective bargaining were indispensable for peaceful industrial relations. In the bituminous coal strike of 1902, when employers refused to meet with employees to discuss grievances, Theodore Roosevelt for the first time used the office of President to force consultation between the two parties. But this action was ceremonial, designed more to demonstrate to the public and to business that government could force peaceful solutions when private parties could not. Only with Woodrow Wilson did an administration embark on a sustained defense of union recognition and collective bargaining. For the first time in history, in the Colorado coal strike (1913–14) President Wilson used federal troops not to protect strikebreakers but to protect property of both parties while they negotiated a settlement. Far more important, the Division of Conciliation, established in the act instituting the Department of Labor, dealt with an increasing number of labor disputes. Such action assumed bargaining between equals, as Secretary William Wilson widely argued and as management agreed by protesting vigorously against the Department's activity. When during World War I the administration recognized unionization and collective bargaining as the proper techniques of industrial relations, its policy came as a logical extension of an approach in force since 1913.

Among different segments of the economy the organizational revolution progressed unevenly. Corporate industry, the first and easiest to come together, controlled far greater resources and commanded far greater influence than did other groups. Distributors, the next most successful in organizing, also constituted powerful elements of the business world; their battles with the railroads were essentially contests within the business community between corporations with different economic functions. The power of both these groups, moreover, depended to a great degree upon the strategic position that they occupied in the price-and-market system. Farm and labor groups, on the other hand, commanding far smaller resources, and relying for their power on numbers rather than on control of crucial sectors of the economy, organized only with great difficulty. Most of all, they faced determined resistance from far more powerful corporate business, which they overcame only gradually and with great difficulty.

Despite these differences in the pace of organization, industrialists, shippers, farm-commodity organizations, and labor unions developed in common a firm commitment to the existing economic order. Whereas in previous years many had expressed dissatisfaction with the "system" and had voiced the conviction that it could be cast aside, the new economic organizations accepted the implications of industrialism and concentrated on working out their destiny within it. Their very success in coping with day-to-day problems through collective action cemented their attachment to the new industrial society.

IV. The Individual in an Impersonal Society

To those sensitive to human values the tendencies of industrialism seemed ominous. Not for a moment would they disavow the benefits of rising industrial productivity; yet they were deeply concerned with the fate of the individual amid this development. Would not the increasing specialization of tasks, the interdependence of the economic network, and the mounting necessity for collective action seriously restrict opportunities for individual economic and political endeavor? Where and how, in such an impersonal society, could one exercise personal responsibility? Did not the increasing emphasis on the acquisition of material wealth distort deeper, human, non-material needs? And what of the millions of people not simply in abject poverty but creatively and spiritually defeated, caught by their environmental circumstances so tightly that they could not maintain a minimum of personal dignity? Many Americans who raised such questions struck out against the confining forces of industrial society and in positive support of reforms that would give meaning to the individual.

The Response to Industrialism

This task was especially critical for organized religion. Prior to the 1890's religious leaders had defended business against attack and had praised economic growth as a product of spiritual endeavor; to be concerned with the spiritual consequences of industrialism required a drastic shift in emphasis. Yet, direct experience with the impact of industrialism on individuals and on society convinced many religious leaders that the new conditions were more a menace than a boon to spiritual values. The declining prestige and authority of religion contributed to this change in attitude. Confined more and more to Sunday and then to Sunday morning, religion became for many more a social affair than a moving experience; even to maintain the Sabbath as a religious day proved to be increasingly difficult. Church membership, especially among workingmen, declined sharply. In the face of the increase in secular learning, religious leaders no longer commanded the moral and intellectual respect of former years; they were replaced as presidents and members of boards of trustees of universities by businessmen, bankers, and lawyers. In a sample of private institutions investigated by one author, 39 per cent of the governing board members in 1860 were clergymen, while by 1930 clergymen comprised only 7 per cent of the same group. The declining relative economic position of ministers, moreover, contributed personal evidence of the fate of religion in industrial America.

Closely related to the reorientation of religion was the active entrance of women into American public affairs between 1890 and 1914. Women's organizations were concerned primarily with problems of the church, the school, and the home; they found common ground with religious leaders both in the search for areas in which to exercise individual moral obligation and in concern for the impact of industrialism on the lives of others. These women's groups were highly articulate and well organized, and their members came mainly from middle- and upper-income groups, where the leisure essential for civic activity was increasingly available. They played an influential role in shaping the course of reform movements in the early twentieth century.

Their national organization, the General Federation of Women's Clubs, was formed in 1890; by 1912 it numbered some one million members. Coming together originally to become more "cultured," more versed in the humanities, the clubwomen soon transformed a shocked distaste for social conditions in their home communities into vigorous nationwide action. Mrs. Sarah Platt Decker, a leading clubwoman of Colorado, where women had held the suffrage since 1893, spearheaded this change in emphasis. Elected president of the Federation at its convention in 1904, Mrs. Decker challenged the delegates: "Ladies . . . I have an important piece of news for you. Dante is dead. He has been dead for several centuries, and I think it is time that we dropped the study of his inferno and turned attention to our own." From that time forward the Federation vigorously pursued a program of reform to protect child and women workers, to improve schools, to further the pure-food movement, and to beautify their communities.

Concern for decreasing individual economic opportunity came from the new urban middle class—clerical workers, salespeople, government employees, technicians, and salaried professionals. This group rose in numbers between 1870 and 1910 from 756,000 to 5,609,000, a far more rapid increase than for the old middle class—business entrepreneurs and independent professional men—for other groups, or for the population as a whole. Not yet reconciled to permanent status as white-collar wage and salary earners, members of the new middle class looked upon their jobs as stepping-stones in advancement to greater independence. Rising in the social scale from either rural or lower-income urban backgrounds, they were on the make; they were buoyed and inspired by the myth that unlimited economic opportunity was available to all, the belief that any man with personal virtues of honesty, thrift, hard work, and sobriety could become economically independent, could "count for something" in the larger economic world. Yet, precisely at the time when the ranks of the new middle class were growing rapidly, the possibilities of realizing the dream of independence were increasing far more slowly. For, more and more, corporate officials rather than individual entrepreneurs held the power to make basic economic decisions; just as wage and salary earners received their paychecks from others, so they carried out orders made by the same employers. The shock of this innovation became as great for the new middle class in the early twentieth century as it had been for labor in the nineteenth. Just as labor's earlier protests proved to be futile, so did the righteous outcries of betrayal with which the new middle class filled the atmosphere of the Progressive Era.

Profound changes in the approach to knowledge stimulated intellectuals, those whose main social role was to produce, disseminate, or manipulate ideas, to engage in reform activity. Before the late nineteenth century, man had acquired knowledge about human affairs primarily by deductive reasoning from assumed principles; he frequently accounted for the origin and nature of institutions in supernatural terms. However, the Englishman Charles Darwin (1809–82), in *On the Origin of Species* (1859) and *The Descent of Man* (1871), explained man's evolution as a product of strictly natural processes and thereby stimulated others to search for natural rather than supernatural explanations of the growth of human institutions. Established truths in history, law, politics, economics, and psychology rapidly came under question. In philosophy William James (1842–1910) and John Dewey (1859–1952) developed pragmatism, a viewpoint which stressed the tentative nature of truth, tested not by logic but by experiment and results. This approach widened enormously the range of human inquiry and knowledge and stimulated a vigorous search for facts by a rising group of young social scientists in the universities. It also seemed to provide the hope, as pioneering sociologist Lester Ward argued, that social science might solve the problems of the industrial age. Combining a professional interest in social science with a deep concern for social betterment, such men as the economist John R. Commons and the sociologist Edward A. Ross contributed actively to the intellectual leadership of early twentieth-century reform.

This new group of intellectuals placed supreme value upon the creative individual, his freedom to develop fully his ideas and to disseminate his views. They abhorred the notion that society was composed basically of groups which struggled to gain power and influence; they were horrified at evidence of class conflict in American life. The basic social unit, so these leaders of thought argued, was the individual, and the fundamental social force was individual human reason. They saw social change "as the work of reformed individuals acting as individuals," more specifically in terms of education and governmental action that would regenerate the individual mind and moral conscience. They conceived of themselves as members of an aristocracy of intelligence that would solve society's ills by educating "the public" and tapping its intelligence as a whole. These new intellectuals provided a rationale and a unifying force for many in the Progressive period who shared their concern for individual reason in social action.

All these—ministers, women, the new middle class, and the new intellectuals—held a deep though often undefined fear that the tendencies of modern industrialism threatened the creative individual. This problem they spoke of as a conflict between material and human values. "Men," complained Rheta Childe Dorr in her book *What Eight Million Women Want* (1910), ". . . believe . . . that material gain and visible reward are alone worth coveting. . . . To the business man capital and labor are both abstractions. To women . . . labor is a purely human proposition, a thing of flesh and blood." Materialism to such leaders meant, not merely the excessive accumulation of wealth, the corruption in business and politics, the objection of businessmen college trustees to the views of college professors, or the measurement of success in terms of money, but more deeply the way in which the new industrial processes tended to impede the expression of individual responsibility and individual striving—the reduction of independent entrepreneurs to wage-earner cogs in bureaucratic industrial machines, the declining attention to religious and moral standards, the helplessness of those in poverty, and the threatening tendency of group struggle to diminish the influence of reason in public affairs. Materialism became the symbol of all the adverse consequences of industrialism.

THE HUMANITARIAN IMPULSE

To the individualist the most shocking fact of modern industrial society was the wretched condition of the urban poor. Although many in the 1870's and 1880's had explained poverty as an unfortunate but necessary element of progress, the early-twentieth-century sensitive individual responded with a feeling of guilt. The mainspring of the humanitarian movement in the Progressive Era lay in a stricken conscience, a sense of shock and shame on the part of individuals who could not live with themselves without acting to improve the condition of the poor. Such an experience and reaction channeled much of the individualistic impulse into urban social reform.

This was especially true of organized Protestantism. Early in the nineteenth century American Protestantism had broken away from a pessimistic, other-worldly Calvinism to emphasize the possibilities of human improvement in this life and to engage zealously in such humanitarian réform as the antislavery movement. Increasing emphasis on salvation in this world led Horace Bushnell (1802–76), among others, to develop the doctrine of Christian Nurture, the view that correct home environment could create Christian character. The argument soon moved one step further to the contention that personal moral regeneration depended upon a favorable environment in the broader society. In *The Freedom of the Faith* (1883) Theodore Munger presented an early systematic statement of this "new theology"; the individual, he argued, was so inextricably entwined in a social network that one could not intelligently save individual souls without first saving society. The social gospel, as the new emphasis became known, completely reversed the traditional view that poverty and vice resulted from inward depravity to argue that those very social conditions caused unchristian character. Yet the new emphasis was social only in its conception of the roots of behavior; its basic concern still lay with individual moral values.

A great number of events in organized religion gave evidence of this new concern for social reform. Washington Gladden, minister of the First Congregational Church in Columbus, Ohio, became the outspoken leader of the social gospel. As early as the 1870's Gladden had begun a lively interest in the question of labor-management relations at a time when such a concern among clergymen hardly gave rise to respect. Although Gladden often criticized trade-union tactics, he clearly agreed with their larger aims; sympathetically he sought from wage earners their attitudes toward the church and toward employers. Gladden tried to steer a middle course on the labor question, arguing that unbridled competition, which placed a premium on the most unscrupulous tactics, was contradictory to

The Response to Industrialism

Christian love. Yet he also attacked radical views, maintaining that the social order should not be "socialized" but Christianized. Popular social gospel novels described the changed attitude toward the poor when people suddenly became Christians. The most famous was *In His Steps*, which a Topeka, Kansas, minister, Charles M. Sheldon, wrote in 1896. In this dramatic novel the minister asked his congregation to make all future decisions in accordance with the question, "What would Jesus have done about it?" By 1933 over 23,000,000 copies of Sheldon's book had been sold. The social gospel movement played an influential role in the new Federal Council of the Churches of Christ in America, formed in 1905; a group of young ministers, for example, John Haynes Holmes and Harry Emerson Fosdick, inspired by the new emphasis in Protestantism, directed the Council toward such social reform movements as labor, minority rights, and international peace.

Urban Christianity everywhere took a new emphasis, even though not always under the influence of a reasoned gospel. "Institutional churches" arose, devoted not only to ministering to the soul but also to creating practical opportunities that parishioners could not obtain elsewhere. Churches provided recreational and educational facilities, first in 1868 at the Grace Episcopal Church in New York. Gymnasiums, libraries, lecture rooms, classrooms, and social rooms became standard necessities for the modern church. The Salvation Army, which General William Booth (1829–1912) founded in England in 1873, ministered to the urban poor on an even more elementary level; it brought aid to millions in the form of food, ice, and coal allotments, employment bureaus, day nurseries, and summer outings. Through such institutional changes as these, urban Protestantism survived when it appeared that its lack of touch with the daily lives of parishioners might create a permanent decline in membership.

The Individual in an Impersonal Society

Closely allied with the organized church movement, though somewhat more secular in tone, was the social justice movement. Composed of intellectuals, ministers, lawyers, and, above all, women, the social justice movement sought governmental means to lessen the impact of industrialism on the less fortunate members of society. The movement comprised organizations such as the National Consumers' League, composed of women who used their power as consumers to force employers to provide more humane labor conditions; the National Child Labor Committee, which worked for state and federal laws to abolish or limit child labor; and the American Association for Labor Legislation, an organization of lawyers and intellectuals which drew up humanitarian labor legislation. Women became extremely active in social justice reforms, especially those who found their careers in the new social work profession and its allied movements. Among the most prominent were Jane Addams (1860–1935), Lillian Wald, Florence Kelley, and Julia Lathrop. Intimately related to all this were the increasingly popular settlement houses in the midst of slums; people of a troubled humanitarian conscience—frequently young college students— went there to experience firsthand the lives of the poor and to take part in social thought and action. The most famous of these, Jane Addams' Hull House in Chicago, became a cultural and inspirational center for the entire humanitarian movement.

Social justice reformers felt special concern for the inability of the urban poor to rise above the grip of economic circumstance, to have faith in themselves, and to improve their lot. The condition of the poor involved a moral problem, one of releasing the creative and spiritual energies of those whom their environment had chained to passivity. This environmental viewpoint greatly modified the emphasis of humanitarian reform from a cold dispensation of charity to an examination and treatment of the causes of poverty; such was the new "scientific" reform, a concern for dealing with causes rather than changing surface conditions. The National Conference of Charities and Corrections, the national center of humanitarian endeavor, in 1915 became the National Conference of Social Work. As its president declared in 1906, the dominant idea of modern philanthropy was "a determination to seek out and to strike effectively at those organized forces of evil, at those particular causes of dependence and intolerable living conditions which are beyond the control of the individuals whom they injure and whom they too often destroy." State and federal governments could modify such environmental conditions through a legislative guaranty of minimum economic standards, the social justice reformers believed. Minimum wages, maximum hours, workmen's compensation, and widows' and children's pensions were all covered in the comprehensive program first formulated by the National Conference in 1912. These minimum standards were intended, not to guarantee livelihood, but rather to afford sufficient security so that the individual could develop incentive to help himself. To reach this objective, social justice leaders sought social means, state and federal action, but their ends remained intensely individualistic, the release of spiritual and creative energy in individual men.

Prior to World War I the social justice movement met greatest success in limiting the working hours of women. After the Supreme Court, in the case of *Muller* v. *Oregon* (1908), upheld an Oregon law restricting the hours of women workers, the National Consumers' League launched a successful nationwide campaign to establish such laws in each state. The drive to secure minimum-wage legislation for women, on the other hand, met determined opposition from the courts, which ruled such laws unconstitutional as a violation of freedom of contract. The local child welfare campaigns accomplished more, producing juvenile courts, recreational facilities, and compulsory school laws. Legislation to limit child labor provoked special controversy. Prior to 1912 the Consumers' League and the National Child Labor Association obtained effective laws in almost every state outside the South, where the main opposition came from the textile industry, which employed many children. Convinced that only a federal law could bring the South to terms, in 1916 the reformers persuaded President Wilson to support such a measure over the opposition of his southern congressional leaders. The Supreme Court soon declared the subsequent Keating-Owen Act unconstitutional; a second attempt in 1917 to frame a law to meet the Court's objections failed to win its approval. Not until the New Deal did reformers secure permanently a national child labor law.

The new humanitarian movement remained predominantly Protestant and Jewish. Pope Leo XIII, in his encyclical *Rerum Novarum* (1891), affirmed the responsibility of the state for social improvement, but few Catholic leaders responded. Father John Ryan, a Minnesota priest, stood out as the foremost leader of a small but increasing minority of social reformers in the Catholic church. Father Ryan's Catholic University doctoral dissertation, published under the title *A Living Wage* (1906), declared that in the distribution of profits the employer-capitalist had no just claim until the employees had received a living wage. Emphasizing environmental causes of poverty, Catholic leaders in 1910 formed the National Conference of Catholic Charities. By 1919 church leaders of advanced views issued a "Bishop's Program" declaring for the major social justice reforms of the day. The same year the National Catholic Welfare Council was organized; it maintained a Department of Social Action in which Father Ryan played a prominent part and which worked for social reform in co-operation with the Federal Council of Churches and the Central Conference of American Rabbis.

The Response to Industrialism

Even though the "scientific humanitarian" stressed the role of environment, he also insisted on strict standards of moral behavior. He wished to abolish prize fighting, gambling, slang, and prostitution, to censor literature and drama, to restrict social dancing, and, above all, to prohibit the use of alcohol. Humanitarians often crusaded against corrupt government to eliminate the prostitution, gambling, and drunkenness closely associated with it. Prohibition became the most spectacular of the humanitarian's moral efforts. Ministers and social justice leaders took up the cause. In the public eye the women's suffrage movement became linked intimately with the antiliquor campaign; and well it might have been, for after women secured the right to vote in local elections in Illinois, local ordinances closed some one thousand saloons. In many respects the individualistic reform movement, arising from urban circumstances, was hostile to the agrarian Populism of the nineties, but in its stress on strict moral behavior it lay squarely in the tradition of rural reform.

The individualist also often shared with the agrarian a *rural fundamentalism*, a belief that life on the farm was morally superior to life in the city. This view arose, not from the sympathy of urban reformers with the farmers' plight, but from their difficulty in finding inspiration amid urban squalor and from a traditional association of individualism with farming. To keep his spirit alive where could the sensitive individual turn? Thomas F. Walsh, a wealthy Colorado mine-owner who resided in Washington, D.C., provided the answer in an article written for the predominantly urban members of the American Forestry Association: true moral inspiration came from the physical vigor of "honest" outdoor labor. "Man's inherent and ineradicable love for the soil [is] one of the strongest traits of human nature," Walsh wrote. "This is our natural taste, while the fascinations of town life are artificial. They do not satisfy our deeper feelings." Urban reformers who responded to such sentiments would not personally have chosen a life of farm toil; yet they clung to the image of the fundamental worth of the yeoman farmer, both as the repository of virtue and as the bulwark of traditional American individualism against an overwhelming tide of hostile forces. In federal land policies, for example, urban "rural fundamentalists" found an opportunity to do battle for the individual; they demanded that western lands be distributed to family farmers alone and not to corporate "monopolies." And they strongly approved Theodore Roosevelt's Country Life Commission (1908), which hoped to find a way to counteract a serious decline in rural population by increasing the attractiveness of country life.

Sustenance could be found not simply in rural life but also in nature. "Men have to go back to Mother Nature for health, strength, independence, integrity and inspiration," declared a correspondent to Myra Lloyd Dock, a Pennsylvania civic leader. Urban civic improvement associations fought to extend the opportunities of urban people to have contact with nature. They campaigned to inaugurate city parks, to improve recreation areas, to develop outdoor art, and to eliminate advertising billboards. In 1904, under the leadership of J. Horace McFarland, a Harrisburg, Pennsylvania, civic leader, these groups joined to form the American Civic Association, dedicated to "the cultivation of higher ideals of civic life and beauty in America . . . and the preservation and development of landscape." Aided by Theodore Roosevelt, whose naturalist writings and activities as a sportsman were well known, they secured laws to preserve a number of areas of natural beauty from commercial use: the Big Trees of California, the Palisades of the Hudson, and an increasing number of state and national parks. Urbanites, seeking areas of natural beauty where they could revive their spirits, played a crucial role in the development of our national park system.

The Response to Industrialism

Increasing reliance upon economic power, which accompanied the organizational revolution, also alarmed those concerned with the fate of the individual in modern industrial society. The unorganized new middle class foresaw its aspirations snuffed out amid the struggle among organized producers—labor and capital—to exact more than their share of the nation's income. The middle-class consumer blamed these groups for the rising cost of living that accompanied the upward trend of prices after 1897. Moreover, such contests among powerful economic organizations threatened the very order of society itself. Memory of the social upheavals of the eighties and nineties hung like a pall over the minds of the articulate public; such events could easily recur, they feared. What future lay in store for that orderly and unified society essential for individual achievement if selfish economic groups dominated the political scene and pushed aside those who wished to act for the "public good"?

The enormous growth of the corporation and its expropriation of the power of economic decision especially alarmed the new middle classes. Stockholders—their number rose from 4,400,000 in 1900 to 8,000,000 in 1917—no longer personally supervised their investments but intrusted them to corporate managers who left the security-owner little influence in company affairs. In life insurance, an increasing form of saving for the middle class which increased from $40.69 per capita in 1885 to $179.14 in 1910, the deferred-dividend contract provided the companies with huge surpluses, "other people's money," which they could and did use as they saw fit. In 1905 the New York Armstrong Committee investigation brought to light the wide use of insurance-company funds to carry out securities operations; and in 1913 the Pujo Committee of Congress re-

84

vealed that interlocking directorates created communities of interest among insurance companies, banking and financial houses, and industrial concerns. These facts persuaded the middle class, just as fewer facts had earlier persuaded Populist farmers, that a financial octopus with headquarters in New York was suffocating economic individualism.

The menace of private economic power seemed even greater because no public agency could restrain it; indeed, the influential role of the corporation in politics indicated that government was the servant rather than the master of business. In economic resources the corporation overshadowed state governments. In 1888, for example, while a major railroad with offices in Boston employed 18,000, had receipts of $40,000,000 a year, and paid its highest salaried officer $35,000, the state of Massachusetts employed 6,000, had receipts of $7,000,000 annually, and paid $6,500 as its top salary. By 1900 corporate organizations even more decisively dwarfed state governments. Small wonder that those who sought to retain individual economic opportunity in a corporate society demanded that the power of the federal government be increased to control business. The best specific policies and precise methods of executing them were not always clear to an aroused public, but of the need for an assertion of federal supremacy over corporate power there could be no doubt. Such a program, it should be emphasized, was intended not to destroy but to preserve individual values. The state should be neither pro-business nor anti-business, but above business, as well as above labor, impartial to all, and especially friendly to the aspirations of the honest, moral, patriotic, hard-working individual—the "public."

The increasing strength of labor unions created fears almost as great as did the rise of corporate power. Those who approached the labor question from an interest in individual values tended to reject the weapons of organized labor. Sympathetic to the movement as a whole because they believed that some improvement in labor conditions was essential to prevent social upheaval, they rarely promoted its use of such techniques as the secondary boycott and the closed shop. Where labor became especially vocal and vehement, they responded with bitter hostility. Jane Addams, for example, spoke of "social justice" for the workingman rather than of his "right" to wage industrial combat; she regarded the labor movement as a "general social movement concerning all members of society and not merely a class struggle." Social justice would come not through struggles for power but as concessions from an enlightened and benevolent government. Labor, moreover, suspected "reformers"; although the Knights of Labor, broad in scope and humane in spirit, had welcomed many into its ranks, the AF of L recognized that the humanitarians were not of them, nor even with them. Gompers in 1896 warned his fellow unionists against the "dangers which lurk in the sophistries of labor's emancipation without the power and influence, the struggles and sacrifices of the trade union movement." In 1912 organized labor shied away from the Progressive party, with its "social justice" labor plank, to support the Democrats, who stood more clearly for trade-union action.

In strife between labor and capital, many were inclined to accept the view of Graham Taylor, professor of social economics at the Chicago Theological Seminary and founder of the Chicago Commons settlement house (1894), that one should "protest against the extreme attitude of either side and . . . stand for the rights of the public as the third and greatest party in industrial struggles." In the seventies employers had argued successfully that labor-management relations were the employers' private responsibility, but the community-wide repercussions of the violent strikes of the eighties and nineties clearly demonstrated their public implications. The "public" therefore demanded that government establish mediation and arbitration machinery to settle disputes. It was not surprising that the first such federal mediation affected the railway industry, where stoppages concerned the public most directly; the Erdman Act of 1898 and the Newlands Act of 1913 originated and perfected machinery for mediation and voluntary arbitration in railway disputes.

Many religious leaders, inspired with the vision of the brotherhood of man, rejected not simply the conflict between labor and capital but the entire practice of economic competition—individual or group; it tended, they argued, to promote social disruption rather than social harmony. Such a spirit permeated Christian socialism, the social gospel, the wide participation of ministers in the Socialist party, and the Nationalist movement that Bellamy's *Looking Backward* inspired. "So long as competition continues to be the ruling factor in our industrial system," the Nationalists announced, "the highest development of the individual cannot be reached. . . ." To achieve economic brotherhood, the "principle of association" should be applied. For many this meant municipal, state, and federal operation of the economic system, especially public utilities. Others hoped to apply the principle to the labor question through fostering consumers' and producers' co-operation. The Knights' emphasis on co-operation attracted to it such leaders of religious and social thought as Washington Gladden and the economist Richard T. Ely. Gladden advocated an "industrial partnership," in which workingmen would receive a fixed share of profits, thereby minimizing employer-employee conflict. Such men, who would have nothing of a class struggle, felt that Christian love could be the instrument of creating and cementing a harmonious society.

Internal social tension persuaded other public leaders to emphasize the need to promote national unity; of these, Theodore Roosevelt became the most outspoken. Decrying the influence of special interests, sectional, economic, or cultural, in American life, Roosevelt demanded a more national approach to the country's affairs and a stronger federal executive to deal effectively with national problems. He frequently called upon the historical images of Alexander Hamilton and Abraham Lincoln, both of whom had asserted the national interest and had used a vigorous federal government toward that end. He feared that American society lay on the brink of disastrous disorder that could be prevented only by a vigorous assertion of the national will. At times he argued that war-inspired nationalistic fervor provided the only path toward moral regeneration and national unity. He also advocated a more orderly direction of internal affairs; his views on this subject, scattered through a variety of speeches and public pronouncements, came by 1912 to be known as the "New Nationalism."

In formulating this view more concisely between 1910 and 1912, Herbert Croly's *Promise of American Life* (1909) especially inspired Roosevelt. Though relatively limited in its audience, this book deeply influenced a few national leaders. Croly described the "great American drift," the tendency for Americans to believe that the nation's problems would automatically solve themselves. Such lethargy, he argued, could lead only to social disruption, for it would permit powerful groups in society full sway to struggle for their private gain and leave the public interest without effective guardians. Croly's book proved to be less a blueprint for the future and more a plea for a strong assertion of the national will to overcome disruptive tendencies in America.

Men like Theodore Roosevelt found the alternative to social disorder in the concept and practice of efficiency, the systematic use of resources—human, natural, and financial—to produce the most possible material goods for the entire nation with the least energy.

The Individual in an Impersonal Society

Competition and group struggle for power produced not efficiency but waste, waste of natural resources, of human lives, of human energy used for selfish ends rather than for the public interest. The social problem could be solved not by quarreling over pieces of the pie but by "baking a bigger pie," by more efficient and greater production so that there would be more to go around. Such leaders conceived of a whole society moving toward a common purpose under the guidance of efficiency, of the ideals of science and technology. Even the process of making decisions in a representative government they considered wasteful. Were not urban governments such, and did not the national Congress enact legislation by logrolling rather than by a considered judgment of the best policy for the nation as a whole? Roosevelt complained to a friend, "I am afraid all modern legislative bodies tend to show their incapacity to meet the new and complex needs of the times."

THE POLITICS OF INDIVIDUALISM

Individualists relied upon the force of human reason and moral conscience to effect their objectives. Although they believed that innate promptings of reason and conscience would turn men toward desirable ends, they doubted that men had sufficient knowledge and experience to arouse them to action. To educate and to exhort, therefore, were the individualists' main techniques of social action. Their most characteristic method was exposure, the revelation and wide diffusion of those facts of industrial life which had produced in them a guilty conscience; they hoped that others would react to the same facts in a similar fashion.

The most sensational literature of exposure consisted of "muckraking" articles that revealed political corruption, dishonest business practices, slum conditions, or urban vice. These accounts appeared widely in the new, cheap, popular magazines of the day—

The Response to Industrialism

McClure's, Munsey's, Cosmopolitan, Collier's, and *Everybody's.* The original muckrakers, so named by Theodore Roosevelt, who accused them of seeking to expose only the most sordid aspects of life, were Lincoln Steffens (1866–1936) and Ida Tarbell (1857–1944). Steffens, an astute and resourceful investigator, covered first a number of city and then state governments for *McClure's,* unfolding a trail of political corruption from East to West. Miss Tarbell, a more painstaking researcher who had specialized in biography, wrote a history of the Standard Oil Company and revealed in detail the practices by which that company had become dominant in the refining business. Once *McClure's* had demonstrated that exposure brought financial returns, many other writers and magazines took up the task, becoming more sensational with the passing years. Thomas Lawson, in *Frenzied Finance,* exposed Wall Street; David Graham Phillips, in the *Treason of the Senate,* described the close connection of industrialists and lawmakers; and Upton Sinclair (1878——), in *The Jungle,* a kind of muckraking novel, laid bare the intolerable working conditions in the meat-packing industry.

A few muckraking pieces were sensational versions of the data systematically compiled by social reformers and legislative commissions. The Consumers' League, for example, undertook extensive studies of factory conditions affecting women and child workers. The Russell Sage Foundation sponsored the comprehensive Pittsburgh Survey begun in 1907 which revealed the twelve-hour day, seven-day week in the steel industry. Legislative commissions collected and published similar facts; the most extensive was the nineteen-volume report on the conditions of child and women wage earners, which Congress authorized in 1907. The federal Children's Bureau (1912) and the Women's Bureau (1921) became centers of influence for reforms; their investigations provided information essential for later action. These accounts revealed low wages, long hours, and dangerous working conditions; their description of the close relationship between pitifully low women's wages and prostitution, especially shocking to the general public, was as sensational as the muckraking stories. The courts as well as legislators felt the impact of this mass of data. In *Mueller* v. *Oregon*, which involved the constitutionality of a law limiting the hours of women workers, Louis Brandeis (1856–1941) presented to the Supreme Court a brief extensively documenting the detrimental effect of long hours on the health of women. In its decision upholding the law, the Court revealed that it had been impressed by this pioneering venture in the field of "sociological jurisprudence."

Literary realism was equally influential in impressing the facts of industrial life upon the American public; in this form of literature, increasingly popular after the turn of the century, writers sought to portray the full range of human experience rather than to romanticize it. William Dean Howells (1837–1920), a pioneer in realism, though willing to illuminate current problems, preferred to portray the "smiling aspects of life." Stephen Crane's (1871–1900) *Maggie, A Girl of the Streets*, on the other hand, was the first blatantly frank account of the urban poor. Many writers, not content merely to let the facts speak for themselves, dramatized the plight of the unfortunate by portraying their characters as putty in the face of irresistible impersonal forces. These "naturalists" included Frank Norris (1870–1902), who wrote *The Octopus* and *The Pit*, novels centering around the production and distribution of wheat, and Theodore Dreiser (1871–1945), whose *Sister Carrie* frankly discussed sex and whose *The Titan* and *The Financier* described a businessman in the grip of his environment. Often distorting reality by overdrawing the sense of hopelessness, the naturalists were motivated by an overwhelming realization of the fate of the individual in an impersonal world but also by the hope that the shock would stir the reader's conscience to action.

To bring about such action, however, existing political parties were inadequate. Political parties were essentially "machines," stressing loyalty to the group, manipulating voters rather than stimulating them to form their own decisions. Parties threatened the exercise of individual rational judgment and symbolized those very forces in modern society which reformers deplored. Individualists, therefore, advocated independent voting. For group-machine politics, moreover, they hoped to substitute a purer democracy; voters should be heard directly in legislative and judicial affairs rather than through delegated conventions, elected representatives, or judges. As instruments of this new democracy, the reformers popularized many electoral and legislative innovations: the direct primary to replace the party convention in selecting candidates for office; the election of senators directly by the voting public rather than by state legislatures; the initiative, in which the people could enact laws in a general election if a sufficient number of voters petitioned to request that a measure be placed on the ballot; the referendum, whereby the legislature referred proposed laws to the electorate for approval; and the recall of elected officials from office by popular vote. These political innovations were advocated in part to eliminate political corruption, in part to obtain legislation that existing political organizations opposed, but also to destroy machine politics and to restore political power to the individual. They could thereby realize on a national scale the "pure" New England town-meeting democracy.

Many individualist reformers supported Senator Robert La Follette (1855–1925) as their candidate for the presidency in 1912; others rallied behind Woodrow Wilson (1856–1924). But Theodore Roosevelt's Progressive party was the most complete political expressiol of the crisis in American individualism. Roosevelt had long since captured the imagination of a large segment of the public. His continued emphasis on the need for spiritual values in a materialistic world, his pronouncements asserting the national and public interest against the special interests of capital or labor, his encouragement of reforms to benefit children and women workers, and his stress upon personal moral values as the basis of civilization had created a following that eagerly gathered around him in 1912 under the "Bull Moose" banner.

Individualist reformers provided the tone, the moral fervor, and the campaign energy of the new party. In the Progressive platform of 1912, for example, appeared a plea for minimum working standards which the National Conference of Social Work had drawn up only a few weeks before; significantly the platform gave only token support to union organization and none at all to those techniques that might make unions more effective. Social justice leaders abounded in the party's organization and as its candidates. For the first time, a major political party recognized women, not only in a pioneering women's suffrage plank but through bringing them into the party organization. Ministers eagerly campaigned for the party from the pulpit. One justified his action by insisting that this was a "non-partisan party," another argued that the party was not a "machine" but merely an "organization," and still a third maintained: "It is not the province of the pulpit to say that any man ought to be elected president but it is the province of every pulpit to say that principles of the Progressive party should guide the nation for the next four years." The entire Progressive party movement became a veritable Protestant religious crusade, a fact revealed in the convention's theme song, "Onward, Christian Soldiers," and in Roosevelt's ringing acceptance speech challenge, "We stand at Armageddon and we battle for the Lord."

V. The Impact of Urban Life

The social and cultural impact of industrialism focused on the city. Growing at a fantastic rate, receiving the full force of the innumerable dislocations of the economic revolution, such urban centers as Boston, New York, and Chicago became seething cauldrons of social change. Here a multitude of different peoples, immigrant and native, faced each other with deep suspicion. Uprooted from traditional and familiar surroundings, each was preoccupied with establishing a new life in a strange and alien society. The continuing gulf between rich and poor augmented a fear that social tension would momentarily erupt into violent disorder. From this turmoil only gradually and sporadically there emerged an urban sense of community, of mutual interest, of civic concern for civic affairs; for the speed of growth did not initially permit the pause essential to concerted action. Rural America, moreover, viewing these sprawling urban monsters with mixed horror and envy, recoiled from an invasion of its traditional values and a threat to its stature; to make its peace with urban America was equally painful.

The Impact of Urban Life

For immigrants the adjustment proved especially difficult. By 1900 they constituted about 40 per cent of the population of the twelve largest cities in the country; another 20 per cent were second generation. Each succeeding wave of immigration outnumbered the previous one: the first, between 1820 and 1860 reached approximately five million, the second, between 1860 and 1890, thirteen and one-half million, and the third, between 1900 and 1930, almost nineteen million. Between 1820 and 1930 over thirty-seven and one-half million people came to America in one of the largest and most significant migrations in the world's history. The first two waves came primarily from northern and western Europe, the British Isles, Germany, and the Scandinavian countries; but the third, from southern and eastern Europe, consisted mainly of Italians, Poles, Bohemians, Russian Jews, and other eastern Europeans.

A variety of circumstances lay behind these migrations. A few immigrants sought political asylum after the revolutions of 1848, escape from military service, or freedom from persecution of Jews in Russia. But by far the largest number came simply to better their economic lot. For years Europeans had viewed America as a land of bountiful resources and unlimited opportunity. Yet most immigrants first learned of the promised land through agents of American employers in search of cheap labor or representatives of American steamship and railroad companies seeking passengers and purchasers of western land. European peasants readily responded to the glowing pictures of the United States painted by these men. A rise in population between 1750 and 1850 had increased the pressure on meager land resources; landlords, moreover, in order to develop larger and more efficient production units, increasingly forced peasants from their soil. Those who suffered from such circumstances did not hesitate to exchange the four-acre plot for an un-heard-of one hundred and sixty acres in America.

Only a relatively small number of immigrants realized this dream; unable to finance their journey further, most became stranded in the larger eastern cities. Boston, New York, Phila-delphia, Pittsburgh, Chicago, Cleveland, St. Louis, and Cincinnati teemed with European peoples. In St. Louis and Cincinnati the Ger-mans predominated; in Boston and New York the Irish; Philadel-phia and Chicago became more cosmopolitan. Here the newcomers found jobs, even though these provided only a meager living. Here they found shelter of a sort. But more important, here lived people like themselves with whom they could feel at home. For initially the immigrant in America experienced intense loneliness; he clung to his countrymen and their familiar old-country ways when he could not comprehend those of the new.

America was strange. Democracy: since he had never experi-enced such a novel idea in Europe, the immigrant could hardly con-ceive of political responsibility. Religion: one encountered here an almost unbelievable variety of faiths, each equally acceptable, and none officially supported; such practices seemed odd especially to Catholics and Lutherans accustomed to a state church. Language: in America one met innumerable strange tongues and people who could not understand one's own language. Customs: in the new country one found little respect for the established, time-honored practices, handed down with reverence and awe from ancestors who lived in the same place, even in the same dwellings, centuries ago. Instead, in America everything was in flux, nothing seemed permanent, and traditions became lost in the midst of rapid change. Certainly the new land was a peculiar place.

In American cities the newcomers encountered difficult condi-tions of life and work. Wages were pitifully low in those jobs, largely unskilled, available to them—construction, railway maintenance, coal mining, and urban public works. Newer arrivals found themselves at the bottom of the job scale; whereas wage levels for Germans and Irish held close to native American standards, for the newer immigrants they remained much lower. The tenement houses which they could afford were unpleasant—large families cramped into one or two rooms, living quarters in basements damp with sewage oozing from faulty systems, no plumbing facilities save for a common basin in the hall, and outside privies the rule rather than the exception. In addition to the discouragement of physical surroundings, the immigrant faced bitter hostility from dominant native Americans. The leaders of business and the professions, as well as white-collar workers recruited from the rural countryside, feared the teeming masses flooding the cities; they hesitated to join with them in common affairs and considered them uncivilized, contributing more to the disintegration of society than to its constructive growth. Although anxious to use the immigrant's labor, they hesitated to accept him on other terms.

In the face of such strange and adverse circumstances, the immigrant sought to strengthen more familiar institutions. Although he had left behind the physical features of the old-country village, he could preserve custom, language, and religion brought to the new land. Through the school, the press, and the religious service, the German language, for example, flourished in both rural and urban America for many decades; the *Sängerfest* and the Turnverein perpetuated German song and German physical culture. So it was among immigrants of every nationality. Above all they held most tenaciously to their religion; under the guidance of a priest, pastor, or rabbi who had come with them, Catholics, Lutherans, and Jews re-established in America the type of service they had known at home.

The Response to Industrialism

But this intense desire to cling to a familiar religion itself created several decades of turmoil within the immigrant community. Newer migrants found that religious practices had changed markedly among their countrymen who had come to America much earlier. To Germans who came in the 1840's, American Lutheranism established by those of an earlier crossing appeared so different that it seemed hardly Lutheran at all; to keep their faith free from the influence of an Americanized religion, they established the independent Missouri Synod. Among Catholics differences became especially acute. Although subject to the same hierarchy in America, Germans, Irish, and Italians each sought to re-establish their church as they had known it, with their own language, their familiar ceremonies, and priests of their own nationality. But since the Irish dominated the American hierarchy, later-arriving Germans and Italians met stiff resistance in their attempt to establish their own brand of the faith. Many American Catholic leaders, in fact, hoped to allay American fears of Catholicism by dropping precisely those elements of religion which stressed foreign characteristics. The issue was squarely joined when Peter Paul Cahensly, leader of a Catholic German Emigrant Aid Society, charged that Americanizing influences had prompted many Catholics to lose the faith; he argued for a church organized on the principle of nationality. When the controversy was finally carried to Rome after years of bitter quarreling, the Pope rejected Cahenslyism and reaffirmed that a truly Catholic church should permit geographical organization alone.

The urban political organization became especially important to the immigrant. The crusading reformer scorned the "machine" as an instrument of corruption and partisan patronage. But to the newcomer it provided the means to obtain aid in an unfriendly world and the opportunity to achieve recognition and success when other avenues to fame and fortune were closed. The corrupt political machine which Cincinnati's "Boss" George Cox (1853–1916) controlled did not concern German voters half as much as did his defense of their desire to enjoy the Continental Sunday or his care that shopkeepers, many of them German, bear a light tax burden. One could trust the boss to help find a job, to provide coal when one was on the point of freezing, to arrange for a funeral, to intercede with the authorities in petty arrests, and to protect the saloon, a chief center of social life. In a society that rejected the immigrant's right fully to belong, the boss remained one of the few sources of power in the community which the foreign-born could reach, and the political machine provided one of the few opportunities for him to rise to a position of influence and prestige.

THE NATIVE AMERICAN RESPONSE

If the immigrant found America strange, the native American viewed the immigrant with even more misgiving. These hordes of newcomers, he thought, maintained strange customs, spoke peculiar languages, dressed oddly, and practiced alien Catholic and Jewish religions; they had not the proper reverence for American values, symbols, and heroes. Moreover, they were intimately involved with the most vulgar and unpleasant features of industrial society. They worked at the most menial jobs, lived in the most repulsive sections of town, frequented the most distasteful dives and bawdy houses (respectable people were far more discreet), had the most revolting personal habits, and appeared to be intimately involved in every outburst of labor unrest. One's home, family, or community could hardly remain safe with such barely civilized people around.

Mrs. Matthew T. Scott, president-general of the National Society of the Daughters of the American Revolution, voiced these fears in 1910, with resounding approval from her audience: "We

The Response to Industrialism

must not so eagerly invite all the sons of Shem, Ham, and Japhet, wherever they may have first seen the light, and under whatever traditions and influences and ideals foreign and antagonistic to ours they may have been reared, to trample the mud of millions of alien feet into our spring." Americans could not separate the strangeness of the immigrant from the strangeness of industrial change; both seemed "foreign." Newer immigrants from southern and eastern Europe, even more different in behavior and more poverty-stricken than were those who had come from northwestern Europe, sharpened the contrast. To separate themselves from such people, Americans of northern and western European ancestry insisted on the distinction between "old" and "new" immigrants.

To protect their way of life from these alien influences, native Americans experimented with a variety of restrictive measures, though these were never as drastic as those imposed upon the Negro by the South during this same period. Some enthusiastically indorsed prohibition and Sunday observance to prevent the spread of such subversive customs as the Continental Sunday of relaxation and entertainment. Throughout its turbulent history the prohibition movement pitted native against foreigner. In 1889 the Wisconsin and Illinois legislatures forbade teaching in foreign languages in the schools. Organized labor sought innumerable laws to restrict employment of unnaturalized foreigners as factory workers; later, as the newcomers began to rise economically, similar laws kept them from white-collar jobs. Some states imposed disabilities upon aliens which seemed intended to be simply discriminatory. New York, for example, in 1908 required aliens to pay $20 for a hunting license, while it cost citizens only $1.

Immigration restriction appeared to many to be the only effective device to eliminate alien influence from American society. In 1894 a group of New Englanders, leaders in the professions and public life,

The Impact of Urban Life

formed the Immigration Restriction League for this purpose. Senator Henry Cabot Lodge, from Massachusetts, was their major spokesman. Joining with labor officials who fought competition from cheaper immigrant workers, the League popularized the literacy test for all immigrants. Avowedly the literacy test was intended to exclude the newer arrivals, the ones most feared, who had received far less education than had northern and western Europeans. In 1897 Congress approved a literacy test which President Cleveland vetoed; when Taft in 1913 and Wilson in 1915 again vetoed similar measures, the House failed by a slim margin to override their vetoes. In 1917, stirred by the fears of national crisis, Congress succeeded in overriding a second Wilson veto. When even the literacy test failed to hold back the tide of postwar immigration, Congress in 1921 and 1924 adopted laws limiting the actual number of newcomers.

Although the presidential vetoes provided the crucial resistance to the literacy test, significant opposition came from other sources as well. The business community, in need of a cheap labor supply, argued that the doors should be kept open. Only in periods of severe economic crisis, such as the depression of the 1890's or the post–World War I years, did fear of labor radicalism temporarily produce business sentiment for restriction. The immigrants themselves stood most consistently against the literacy test. Such organizations as the German-American Alliance and the Ancient Order of Hibernians became increasingly active after 1906. Republican politicians, acutely conscious that Italian, Slavic, and Jewish voters contributed enormously to their urban strength after 1894, hesitated to alienate this support. When William Randolph Hearst (1863–1951) in his 1906 race for the New York governorship threatened to dislodge these nationality groups from the Republican party, President Roosevelt countered by appointing a Jew, Oscar Straus (1850–

1926), as Secretary of Commerce and Labor, the federal agency which administered immigration laws. Though these forces retarded the progress of anti-immigrant legislation, they could not prevent its eventual success.

The intellectual leaders of restriction formulated a theory of racial superiority to justify and explain their actions. Americans had long cherished their Anglo-Saxon background, had attributed their flourishing society to superior Anglo-Saxon institutions, and had waxed enthusiastic over their "manifest destiny," their duty to carry their way of life to the rest of the world. Under the impact of social crisis in the 1890's and the fear of alien threats to American society, these optimistic views hardened into a desperate racial vindictiveness which stressed a more clear-cut race superiority. Racists took up the growing study of genetics, soon attributing inherent inferiority especially to the newcomers from southern and eastern Europe. Such views found acceptance among those long concerned with the role of Negroes and Orientals in American life. In 1916 Madison Grant, a wealthy New York patrician, sportsman, and genealogist who dabbled in biology and eugenics, published the fullest expression of racial superiority yet written in America; his book *The Passing of the Great Race* defended racial consciousness, chided his fellowmen for believing that environment could somehow overcome heredity, and warned that the new immigration threatened the purity of northern European stock.

While restrictionists struggled to limit immigration, a movement to assimilate the newcomers into American society took increasing momentum. Social reformers and humanitarians, for example, Jane Addams and Lillian Wald, especially sought to soften the impact of adjustment to a harsh and alien society. In settlement houses in the midst of slums they lived and learned firsthand of immigrant life, encouraged the newcomers to express their own culture, and tried to persuade Americans to appreciate the unique contributions that foreign peoples could make to their community. Composed largely of college students anxious to give expression to Christian values in a complex industrial world, these settlement houses became centers from which the positive qualities of immigrant life were interpreted to the wider community. Their activities produced little of the spectacular, nor did they accomplish much immediately; yet they served to moderate the trend toward greater cleavage between native American and immigrant peoples.

To patriotic societies, the Daughters of the American Revolution, for example, assimilation meant something far different: that the immigrants should give up their ways and fully adopt American customs. Their method of Americanization consisted of exhorting immigrants to be loyal citizens and to submit willingly to the dominant patterns of culture they found here. Numerous organizations arose to further these citizenship activities; their major impulse lay not in humanitarian concern but in a fearful desire to secure conformity to established customs. In 1908 a group of Boston businessmen formed the North American Civic League for Immigrants, originally intended to protect the newcomers from unscrupulous bankers, steamship captains, and fellow countrymen; gradually, however, it became more clearly a body designed to protect businessmen against labor radicalism. Miss Frances Kellor, a leading figure in Americanization, in 1912 persuaded the Progressive party to propose federal action to promote the immigrant's assimilation, education, and advancement; later she prevailed upon a few wealthy backers to finance a Division of Immigrant Education within the federal Bureau of Education. During the heightened nationalism of World War I, this drive to create "good citizens" quickly evolved into a crusade for social conformity and a bitter hostility toward those who failed to respond.

Such campaigns, however, helped little to bridge the gap between native and immigrant communities. Americanizers undoubtedly taught many new citizens the English language and knowledge about American government, but the excesses of the war-borne drive for conformity—in Iowa the governor outlawed the use of all foreign languages even over the telephone—only stimulated a more intense nationalism among the newcomers. Though suppressed during World War I, this resentment flared out as soon as the conforming pressures of national crisis ceased. The process of adjustment came more slowly and with less conscious direction. Second-generation immigrants, not experiencing the same shock of change as did their parents, readily took on many ways of the new country, the language, manners, games, and dress. The tendency of immigrant children to learn English and to adopt American customs, while creating heart-rending conflicts within families, narrowed the gap between native and newcomer.

MUNICIPAL REFORM

Amid the turmoil of cultural adjustment rapid growth created many problems for the entire urban community. Such questions as city health and sanitation, fire and police protection, recreational and educational facilities, heat, light, communication, and transportation became increasingly acute. Solution of these problems required a more effective, positive city administration that could tackle community affairs and draw for its support upon a sense of common concern for mutual problems. The story of urban evolution in the Progressive Era is a tale of the gradual growth of civic pride in a well-run and useful city government.

Such a sense of community emerged only slowly from many particularistic interests, each most preoccupied with its own welfare.

The Impact of Urban Life

Seeking self-protection in a strange world, immigrants were not prone to scruple over the honesty of those who gave them aid; urban reformers they eyed with deep suspicion. Party politicians cared more for the spoils of politics, for patronage, bribery, and corruption than for effective urban government. Dominant city leaders—businessmen, lawyers, ministers—shunned public life; they would not soil their hands with the dirty business of politics, which belonged to the poorer and less successful citizens who could not earn their bread by honest toil. Individual businessmen, both those who managed large public utility corporations and those who were door-to-door peddlers, conceived of the city aldermen more as a source of purchasable legal favors than as officials responsible to the public.

Among these "special interests" gas, electric, and street-railway corporations were the most powerful and most aggressive; they played a dominant role in corrupting city councils. To be safe, they lavishly contributed funds to both parties and bought state legislators as well as city aldermen. Charles T. Yerkes (1837–1905), for example, after a notorious career in Philadelphia, moved on to the Chicago street-railway business, where he dominated a corrupt city council for a decade. After fleecing the elite of Chicago in a clever traction deal, he hastened to England to try his hand at the London tube. Earlier he had "atoned" for his chicanery in the Windy City with a gift to the University of Chicago to establish the famous Yerkes Observatory at Lake Geneva, Wisconsin. Men like Yerkes flourished in the midst of public indifference and venal city aldermen; they exchanged franchises of enormous value for "boodle," funds which ward leaders could well use to maintain their power. Revelations of the political operations of utility corporations aroused the public to demand reform in city government. Yet they constituted only the most powerful and spectacular—because their funds were greater—of a host of "special interests" which inhibited the growth of effective urban administration.

In the nineteenth century taxpayers had formed the backbone of the municipal reform movement. Tired of contributing funds that found their way into corruption, these middle- and upper-class property-holders had spearheaded sporadic drives for honest officials in Brooklyn, Cleveland, and elsewhere, only to discover that soon the reformers needed reforming. The twentieth-century movement, more sustained and successful, stressed not simply efficiency but increased expenditures and increased tax rates to finance needed city services. The civic consciousness that lay behind this movement contributed, in addition to mere interest in one's pocketbook, a growing concern for an orderly and attractive urban community. Yet this impulse could not triumph alone. For even though an aroused civic pride set the tone of municipal reform, it depended on far less attractive influences for its victory. The fight against Yerkes in Chicago succeeded only because Mayor Carter Harrison, Jr., brought to his support corrupt aldermen who were furious for not having received a "fair" share of the boodle. The utilities themselves contributed to their undoing by demanding longer-term franchises, less frequently subject to annoying aldermanic demands for graft; in the face of this threat to their source of funds, the politicians eagerly helped to bring the utilities to terms. Amid such jockeying for advantage, and under the leadership of men who knew how to beat the "machine" at its own game, reform emerged the victor.

To reformers concerned with more effective urban government, partisan politics hindered more than helped; therefore, they sought ways to free municipal affairs from the consequences of party struggles and to encourage the direct expression of civic concern.

To bypass existing political machinery, they advocated direct nominations of candidates for office, the secret, or Australian, ballot, and separation of local and national elections. Through the initiative and referendum they hoped to establish a means directly to express the public will when it was thwarted by the council or legislature. Such reforms arose not from great faith in existing democracy—in fact, they reflected distrust of the current electorate—but from the hope that a new civic spirit could destroy the particularistic roadblocks to civic growth. For exactly the same reason many urban leaders, Frederic C. Howe of Cleveland, for example, demanded that the city own and operate its utilities; municipal ownership would eliminate corruption, partisan strife, and the influence of utility corporations from a major area of civic affairs, but it would also arouse and sustain public pride in effective municipal action. The municipal ownership movement which flourished around the turn of the century arose not from a reasoned socialistic philosophy but from an attempt to implement the objectives of urban reform.

Efficient urban administration also required innovations in the organization of government. The typical two-house legislative body, the elective mayor with limited powers, and executive officers over whom the mayor held no control encouraged buck-passing and irresponsibility. To force officials to be accountable for their acts, reformers fought to establish clearer lines of authority and to increase the mayor's power to appoint his subordinates and to initiate policy. Some cities experimented with more drastic innovations in which the council hired a city manager to administer affairs or appointed a commission with full executive powers. To effect such reforms, municipalities were forced to seek additional control over their own affairs from state legislatures; the latter, however, were hostile to the cities. Dominated by rural lawmakers who were suspicious of all things urban, state legislatures also proved susceptible to influence from those very corporations which sought to prevent municipal reform. When Charles T. Yerkes could not obtain favorable utility ordinances from Chicago aldermen, for example, he persuaded Illinois state legislators to enact measures which would accomplish the same purpose. The fight for effective city government, therefore, moved frequently to the state capitol and took the form of a struggle for municipal home rule, for a new state municipal code which would grant cities the power and authority to cope with their own problems.

Innumerable new organizations sought to better city government. In 1894 they joined in a nationwide information clearing house, the National Municipal League; under the direction of Clinton Rogers Woodruff, its secretary for twenty-five years, the League inspired urban improvement on a front as wide as urban growth itself. Chambers of commerce contributed heavily to the drive for a more equitable urban tax burden, better utility service, and more effective municipal government. The American Civic Association, formed in 1904, spearheaded the drive for urban recreational facilities. To the public mind, however, the persistent struggle by these groups was overshadowed by a few spectacular episodes. Such mayors as Hazen Pingree of Detroit, Samuel "Golden-Rule" Jones and Brand Whitlock of Toledo, and Tom Johnson and Newton Baker of Cleveland achieved a notoriety battling the "machine" which often led to a larger political career. Their fight for a better city inspired many throughout the country but obscured the contributions of a vast number of unsung heroes.

The issues that especially occupied the attention of municipal reformers were tax equalization and public utility control. Tax problems arose from the generous favors which both states and cities, in their first stage of growth, had granted public utilities; lower property assessments and lower taxation rates especially aided railroad construction. These concessions now seemed to be glaring inequities. In Jersey City, for example, although the average property tax rate was $28 per $1,000, the railroads paid nothing to the city on their main-line real estate, personal property, and franchises and only $15 per $1,000 on other property. It was estimated in 1900 that the railroads in New Jersey bore only one-third of their just tax burden. Facing the increasing load of municipal debt, urban property owners demanded that railroads pay taxes at the same rate as did others. Although equalization proceeded under such pressure, it came only after a bitter struggle in the legislature and often as a partial victory.

A more comprehensive attack took place on those gas, light, and street-railway utilities which provided city services. Affecting intimately the lives of all urban citizens, the utility seemed to be an impersonal, greedy octopus; it had rarely been popular. Revolted by their unsightliness and noise, property owners had bitterly resisted street-railway extension and especially the elevateds. Hostility grew when equipment became motorized and motormen used to horsecar operations now gleefully careened through the streets; in Brooklyn, where street-railway fatalities reached one per week in 1886, the baseball team acquired the nickname, the "Trolley Dodgers." Revelations of case after case of fraud and bribery involving aldermen and utilities only provided the last straw for a public already none too friendly to the corporations. When many franchises became subject to renewal around the turn of the century, reform groups insisted that their terms severely limit utility practices and increase remuneration to the city. Outright municipal ownership often appeared to be the only logical solution. Elsewhere state commissions were established carefully to prescribe rates and standards, first in Wisconsin in 1906, in New York the following year, and thereafter in many other states.

The Response to Industrialism

THE DEFENSE OF RURAL LIFE

The new urban centers profoundly altered small-town and rural patterns of culture. Country people envied the increasing population, wealth, and power of the cities, but they also feared the strange new interests and activities which urban leisure made possible, as well as the institutions which arose among immigrants. Such innovations reached out to assert themselves in the wider life of the state and nation and to transform the dominant rural-rooted traditions of the entire country. Farming communities felt that their mode of living, what they considered to be the traditional American way of life, was threatened.

The rural voter opposed much of the urban civic reform movement; political support for state laws to solve municipal problems came largely from the cities. Thinking that "it was a healthy thing to give the rural districts a check on the 'slick city fellows,' " farmers looked upon municipal home rule with suspicion. In state after state they voted against laws to aid labor; they opposed other humanitarian reforms such as the abolition of capital punishment; they defeated the centralization of state functions to streamline administration, lest it shift control from rural to urban areas; they opposed the initiative and referendum when they felt that these would further municipal reform without aiding rural interests. In the Ohio election of 1912, for example, rural areas opposed twenty-six out of forty-two constitutional amendments which urban reformers desired.

Rural voters could exercise considerable influence because they held political power increasingly out of proportion to their numbers. Such power came through a lag in the apportionment of legislators in state assemblies; based upon an earlier distribution of population, representation did not change to conform to the rapid growth of cities. Long after urban areas outnumbered rural in such states as Illinois, Ohio, New York, and Massachusetts, the country-side continued to retain political control of state legislatures and could there register an effective protest against the innovations it distrusted. Farmers, moreover, bitterly opposed attempts to grant cities a representation more equal to their share of the population.

Early in the twentieth century civic leaders demanded that rural areas co-operate to improve the facilities of the entire state by creating better rural highways and rural schools and by improving agricultural practices. The Country Life Movement unified all these attempts at rural advancement; it sought to apply to the countryside ideals of civic responsibility first established in urban centers. These rural problems came forcefully to public attention around the turn of the century when farm population declined noticeably and many farms were abandoned. Led by Professor Liberty Hyde Bailey of Cornell University, ministers, agricultural college specialists, educators, and other civic leaders initiated a program to make rural life more attractive and more profitable, to bring to farming areas the benefits of urban communities, and to forestall a decline of agrarian population. The movement received official sanction and considerable aid when in 1908 Theodore Roosevelt sponsored the Country Life Commission to investigate rural living; as its chief task the Commission compiled information about farm life and publicized the entire movement.

Country Life leaders especially encouraged scientific farming. For many years the state agricultural colleges and experiment stations had promoted agricultural science, but rarely had they sought to educate farmers to apply their discoveries. Much could be accomplished, it was thought, if each county maintained an agricultural expert to disseminate technical advice. A New York county established the first such expert or agent in 1912. The idea spread rapidly; in the Smith-Lever Act in 1914 the federal government provided grant-in-aid funds to render the plan permanent and available to every county in the nation. The program grew especially under the intense pressure for increased production during World War I.

To raise the standards of rural education, reformers worked to consolidate schools, to improve teacher training, and to adapt courses to the needs of farm youth. State and local groups promoted school consolidations, while the program for agricultural education received federal grants-in-aid to the states in the Smith-Hughes Act of 1917. The good-roads movement, closely intertwined with these developments, sought to increase state and local funds to construct hard-surfaced roads and to streamline road administration under a state highway commission. Automobile transportation, many felt, would create a more attractive rural life.

These programs did not arise from a mass movement of farmers; a few rural leaders and urban groups with a stake in rural affairs advanced them. Inspiration and leadership for them came from the state agricultural colleges throughout the country. Agitation for agricultural education and scientific agriculture arose from urban groups that had a stake in agricultural prosperity—railroads concerned with the decline in farm railroad traffic, merchants who feared the shrinkage of rural markets, and bankers worried about the possible loss of borrowers. These groups not only financed the original county-agent movement; they spearheaded the drive for federal aid. Through chambers of commerce urban merchants joined with urban automobile enthusiasts to boost the good-roads movement. Educational organizations which reflected the new interests arising from the improved urban school sought to raise the standards of entire states through a vigorous rural education program.

The Impact of Urban Life

Though such efforts ultimately increased the standard of rural life, farmers initially considered them to be an alien attempt to transform their traditional patterns of living. The state highway commission, farmers suspected, would shift control from county road officials and place greater emphasis on thoroughfares between metropolitan centers rather than on the farm-to-market roads that rural people preferred. School consolidations threatened to destroy one of the most revered centers of rural society, the one-room school, and to place school affairs in the hands of town and city officials who had little understanding of rural ways of life. And the movement for scientific farming would replace traditional patterns of agriculture with strange and impractical ideas hatched in some head or laboratory far removed from the realities of farming. These new ventures not only menaced rural institutions but, inspired and directed by outsiders, threatened to transfer control of rural affairs from farmers to urban strangers. Rural people were deeply concerned about their loss of influence in the civic revival.

Farmers not only resisted these urban-inspired attacks on their way of life; after the depression of 1893–97 they undertook a counteroffensive. Rural areas vigorously supported legislation to restrict immigration in order to preserve native American culture from contamination by foreign influences. Similar motives lay at the root of the rural-based fundamentalist movement; reacting against the more liberal interpretation of the Bible and the increasing urban social concerns of the church, orthodox religious leaders restated the fundamental beliefs of Christianity. Within numerous denominations rural church leaders fought to turn back the tide of a more critical attitude toward authority as a source of truth. Although this reaction began as early as 1876 when the annual Niagara Bible Conference began, it grew in intensity in the early twentieth century. In 1909 two California oil millionaires financed a restatement of this

The Response to Industrialism

view, *The Fundamentals: A Testimony to the Truth*, that quickly sold three million copies. The most colorful figure in the new crusade, the evangelist Billy Sunday (1863–1935), used a host of dramatic and unorthodox tactics to fill with fervor thousands in small-town and rural America.

The antiliquor movement, which assumed increasing strength in the early years of the twentieth century, became the most effective rural offensive action against the urban invasion. Although this movement did not originally arise from rural-urban tension (its inspiration came from leaders in both areas), it concentrated its attack on the urban saloon and urban inebriates. The enemies of alcohol argued that the main evil of municipal government lay in a corrupt alliance between politicians and saloonkeepers. Moreover, the major political support for prohibition came from rural areas; the Anti-Saloon League, a political arm of the Protestant churches, consciously sought to arouse the rural vote for its program because it well knew that it could rely on only a minority of voters in the cities. The dominant urban religious groups, Catholic and Jewish, were indifferent or openly hostile to prohibition. Urban reformers, in fact, even though friendly to restrictions on drinking, often suspected that their opponents encouraged this issue to turn attention from needed urban reforms and to obtain strength in rural areas to defeat urban innovations. In many states the wave of urban reform receded in a rural reaction dominated by a demand for prohibition.

The Anti-Saloon League, organized in 1895, soon led the antiliquor crusade; it formed a disciplined political machine, thoroughly non-partisan, to which congressmen paid increasing attention. In states predominantly rural the League moved to establish state-wide prohibition; beginning with Georgia in 1907, at least fourteen states of the South and West enforced prohibition by 1916. Where the League could not secure state-wide restrictions, it pushed through local option, and by 1914 had largely dried up rural America. After having obtained the Webb-Kenyon Act in 1913, which prohibited interstate shipment of liquor into states in violation of the local law, the League set out to capture the last stronghold of liquor—the cities—by nationwide prohibition. This it obtained in the Eighteenth Amendment in 1920. Despite vain protests in favor of "personal liberty," rural Protestant America at last subdued the urban menace to its traditional morals and culture.

VI. Protest from the South and West

Economic growth proceeded at an uneven pace in the different sections of the country. Although the South and the West experienced the same industrial influences as did the Northeast, conditions peculiar to their areas retarded development. In part the differences lay in inherent economic disadvantages; but they also stemmed from the fact that northeastern policies tended to restrict the South and West to a colonial economic pattern as a source of raw materials and markets for northeastern industry. Economically and psychologically, southern and western aspirations for growth lay under the shadow of a far more advanced section that possessed the power to make both private and public decisions in its own interest and detrimental to others. Underdeveloped areas increasingly called upon the federal government for aid in economic growth, for elimination of those policies which they considered especially favorable to the Northeast, and for new laws to restrict the power of northeastern economic leaders to set the pattern of regional economic progress. Sectional economic conflict ran deep during the Progressive Era and produced widespread political repercussions.

Protest from the South and West

Abundant natural resources provided the impetus for the initial stage of western economic growth. Agriculture arose early in the rich valleys of the Pacific states. The cattle industry, springing up in Texas in the 1850's, moved northward to the luxurious range-lands of the prairies and plains; the rich soils of the Middle Border, from the Dakotas to Oklahoma, soon supported thriving wheat fields. Much of the vast timber tracts in the Rockies, the Sierra Nevadas, and the Cascades would remain inaccessible for decades, but those of the Pacific Northwest began to produce lumber for the national market once the Great Northern reached Seattle in 1893. Gold, silver, and copper deposits in California, Nevada, Montana, Colorado, and Arizona gave rise to a vigorous mining industry.

Federal policies encouraged rapid exploitation of these resources by encouraging land to pass easily from federal ownership into private hands. The Homestead Act of 1862 granted free 160 acres to any family that would occupy it; settlers obtained even more farms through purchasing from railroads parcels of their federal grants. One could obtain land under the Timber Culture Act of 1873 if he planted trees on it, and under the Desert Land Act of 1877 if he undertook irrigation; under the Timber and Stone Act of 1878 one could secure materials to aid in building construction. Federal agricultural land sales, still at the minimum auction price of $1.25 an acre, also proceeded rapidly. Moreover, Congress disposed of mineral and timber lands at similar prices; a Mineral Land Act in 1872, for example, provided for sales at $2.50 to $5.00 an acre irrespective of the quality or quantity of minerals underground. Lax enforcement of these laws permitted even easier resource acquisition; by filing false affidavits one could readily acquire valuable minerals or timber free under the homestead laws. At the same time, the absence of federal laws for the public range permitted cattlemen to exploit federally owned native grasses free and to develop a vigorous western cattle industry.

Many factors peculiar to the West, however, retarded its expansion, and most important among these was the shortage of rainfall. Save for the Pacific Coast and portions of the Rocky Mountain region, the area received less than twenty inches a year. The windmill, which furnished power for raising well water, soon solved the problem of domestic supply. But an adequate amount for agriculture proved far more difficult to obtain. In the 1890's H. W. Campbell partially solved the problem when he developed a system called "dry farming," consisting of new methods of cultivation to preserve moisture. Irrigation, however, became a far more important technique. Begun by settlers as early as the 1850's, the practice of irrigation spread widely, growing from merely diverting streams onto farmland to constructing reservoirs to hold spring flood waters for use later in the year. Irrigation, however, increased production costs, which grew as storage and diversion systems became more elaborate. These high costs, in turn, placed western agriculture under economic handicaps and diverted western farming into truck, fruit, and nut crops which produced a high return per acre.

Inadequate transportation equally hampered western growth. Eastern agriculture had always enjoyed readily available water routes to its markets; here the railroad merely supplemented an already existing transportation network. The West, however, distant from markets, and with almost no satisfactory river navigation, depended solely on the railroad for its growth. Although less acute for the Pacific Coast, which had access to river and ocean transport, the problem was serious on the landlocked prairies, plains, and mountains. Difficulties inherent in western development, however, persuaded private investors to hesitate to construct western railroads;

the West, therefore, called upon the federal government to stimulate its economy by granting lands to private railroad corporations. Five transcontinental lines enjoyed varying amounts of public land grants. Despite the coming of the railroads, the lack of cheaper water transport, especially for heavy materials, continued to place the West at an economic disadvantage relative to other sections.

Once established, the railroads provided significant entrepreneurial leadership for the entire West. Since they preceded settlement, western roads were forced to stimulate economic activity in order to insure the large volume of traffic that would render their enterprises profitable. Initially they concentrated on promoting settlement; immigration agents combed the East and Europe for recruits, offering them attractive terms of transportation and land purchase. James J. Hill (1838–1916), of the Great Northern, pioneered in agricultural promotion; other transcontinentals soon followed his lead in financing educational work in dry farming, in working for state and national legislation to facilitate development, and in co-operating with local and federal officials to encourage irrigation and more stable grazing conditions on the public domain.

Federal ownership of a large portion of the West's natural resources often adversely influenced that area's economic growth. For Congress rarely provided for orderly development and use of the property which came under its jurisdiction, and the states, with few exceptions, could not constitutionally legislate concerning federal property. Absence of even the most elementary methods for determining legal rights to the use of resources forced enterprisers to provide their own protection from interlopers and frequently led to violence. Western economic development entailed a degree of confusion in property titles which other sections did not experience.

Water use posed the most perplexing problem. Water scarcity demanded a set of legal arrangements far different from eastern law that sufficed in an area of relative abundance. Most western states established the doctrine of prior appropriation—first come first served. Anyone could establish a legal claim to water use by posting a notice at the point of diversion and filing a statement with the county clerk. As the demand for water grew, conflicts in its use increased. But when an owner sued to defend his rights, the courts did not know how much water was available and consequently often distributed rights far in excess of the amount actually in existence. Since decisions were invariably appealed to higher courts, suits proved to be costly; moreover, victory in one case did not protect the claimant against other users who might later question his rights. Settlers, therefore, often substituted extralegal armed force for drawn-out, expensive litigation. In 1888 Wyoming pioneered in a more orderly system in which a state engineer measured the available supply and clearly determined and enforced priorities. Although other states did not adopt the same methods, they worked toward more effective laws which provided for orderly development and use of their most critical resource.

Use of the public range became even more chaotic. On millions of acres of federal lands one could freely graze cattle and sheep without restrictions; here again it was first come, first served, with its inevitable conflict. Cattlemen vied with each other for use of the limited grasses; farmers, moving westward, sought to stake out farms on the range against bitter opposition from cattle owners; in the late 1880's sheep moved onto western lands, intensifying competition. On the defensive, cattlemen fenced their traditional ranges with barbed wire; the federal government in 1885 ordered the fences removed. Warfare between cattlemen and sheepherders and between both and settlers led to innumerable outbursts of violence, stampedes, and murders. The most famous incident was the Johnson County, Wyoming, "War" of 1893, in which promiment cattlemen invaded the center of opposition to them in Johnson County, killed two men, and in turn were besieged on a ranch by the aroused community. Federal troops finally rescued the cattlemen and restored order. Cattlemen took the initiative in seeking a federal program to promote more orderly use of the range. They demanded that the government lease range and limit its use to the number of animals which could be grazed safely. Such a measure, to insure stability in range use and incidentally to permit a more orderly and sustained growth of forage, appeared first in 1885. Although the administration of Theodore Roosevelt (1901–9) actively supported the bill, sheepmen and settlers fought it off successfully until Congress in 1934 passed the Taylor Grazing Act.

SOUTHERN ECONOMIC GROWTH

Southern economic development labored, not so much under inherent physical handicaps of climate and distance from markets as did the West, but under restraints imposed by its earlier agrarian patterns of life and its late industrial growth. The South lacked capital, vigorous business leadership, and a skilled labor force; these shortcomings were often closely connected with pre–Civil War King Cotton. When it appeared that the South might industrialize shortly after the War of 1812, the rise and expansion of its cotton-slave economy absorbed most of its entrepreneurial energy and economic resources and stifled industrial activity. To overcome this agrarian orientation became not only a task of diverting resources to other forms of economic endeavor but also of creating a psychological atmosphere favorable to industrialization; this problem the West rarely had to face. The Civil War contributed enormously to this development by discrediting the prewar direction of the South's economy and by permitting men of a different frame of mind to assume leadership.

The Response to Industrialism

The 1880's witnessed the first major impact of the industrial revolution on the South. After the end of Reconstruction in 1877, southern energies turned toward industrial growth. As the depression of the 1870's began to clear in 1878, northern and British capitalists looked with favor upon southern investment opportunities. Southern promoters, in turn, tried to attract capital by offering cheap credit, low taxes and tax exemptions, municipal subsidies, cheap labor, tacit commitments to wink at wage-and-hour laws, and an enthusiastic public. The new southern state governments, which seemed more stable and inclined to retrenchment in state finances, appealed to potential investors. The new turn of events appeared even during the depression when Congress in 1876 repealed the Southern Homestead Act of 1866; this act had reserved all federal land in the South for homestead entries. In Florida, Alabama, Mississippi, Louisiana, and Arkansas, where the federal government owned almost one-third of the area, the new law stimulated extraction of lumber, coal, and iron resources. Southern states, moreover, lavishly conveyed state-owned lands to prospective industrial promoters. By 1884, in fact, the Florida legislature had given away twenty-two million acres of state land even though it owned only fifteen million!

Although the lack of railway transportation did not hamper the growth of the cotton South, it did retard extraction of the region's industrial raw materials and the growth of manufacturing itself. The coming of the railroad, therefore, marked a crucial stage in southern industrial growth. Prior to the Civil War railroad construction lagged, but in the 1880's mileage grew from 16,605 at the beginning of the decade to 39,108 at the close; while the nation's trackage grew 86.5 per cent, that of the South advanced 135.5 per cent. Two factors retarded the integration of this network with that of the entire nation: the difficulty of penetrating the Appalachian barrier, and the three-inch difference in gauges of southern and northern lines. By 1892, however, three successful mountain crossings had been completed south of the Potomac, and in 1886 the Louisville and Nashville Railroad pioneered in moving both rails and wheels the necessary three inches to integrate its line with the northern network.

As in the West, railroads actively promoted the development of the South. The Louisville and Nashville, for example, which owned more than a half-million acres in central Alabama, was instrumental in building up the Alabama mineral region; its president, Milton H. Smith, directed some $30 million in investments toward that area over a twenty-year span. Railroads also took the lead in promoting immigration into the South through their own agents and through state immigration bureaus. The Missouri Pacific and Iron Mountain system, which owned one million acres in Arkansas, employed some three hundred immigration agents in the Northeast and in Europe to secure settlers for these lands. The major southern colonizer, however, was the North American Land and Timber Company, a British corporation which purchased enormous areas of land along the Louisiana Gulf Coast. Pioneering in new methods of rice production, this company enabled Louisiana to become the nation's foremost rice-producing state. These immigration efforts, however, brought no net increase in the South's labor force; in fact, more left the region than came.

Iron, tobacco, and cotton manufacturing stood out as the major accomplishments of the South's industrialization. The iron industry thrived on the economic advantage of rich deposits of iron and coal in very close proximity. By 1898 Birmingham, not founded until 1871, had become the largest shipping point for pig iron in the country and the third largest in the world. The rapid rise of the Alabama iron and steel industry alarmed northern producers, who took steps to retard its growth. Mechanization in the tobacco industry proceeded apace; under the leadership of such new men as James B. Duke (1856–1925), the industry was shifted from Virginia to North Carolina and entered upon a period of vigorous growth. But the rise in cotton textile manufacturing symbolized most dramatically the new industrial South. Although the cotton mill had appeared earlier, its growth in the 1880's proceeded far more rapidly. Located primarily in the Carolinas, Georgia, and Alabama, the industry pioneered in the most modern machinery and the use of electricity. In the 1890's, while the number of the nation's mills increased only 7.5 per cent, those in the South increased 67.4 per cent. Yet the higher profits of southern textile manufacturing rested as much upon the extremely low wages of southern factory workers as on other conditions.

The growth of southern manufacturing, however, only permitted the region to keep pace with the rest of the nation. In view of the lack of industrial growth in previous years, this was a remarkable achievement. Yet even more significant was the change in atmosphere of the South, the spirit of industrial progress which typified the "New South." Newspaper editors played an important role in creating this new spirit: Richard H. Edmonds, who founded the *Manufacturers' Record* in Baltimore in 1882; Henry Grady of the *Atlanta Constitution;* and "Marse" Henry Watterson of the Louisville *Courier Journal*. A number of southern cities held expositions to boost the South. Atlanta, for example, held an International Cotton Exposition in 1881, and Louisville and New Orleans sponsored similar events in 1883 and 1885. The region even spawned its own manuals on the morals and manners of business. In 1885, for example, the Southern Methodist Publishing House brought out the *Law of Success*, based upon the lives of twelve hundred successful men, primarily self-made southerners.

Protest from the South and West

Although farming remained the dominant economic occupation of the South, agriculture failed to advance rapidly. During the Populist-Progressive Era the region still suffered from lack of farm mechanization and from absentee ownership and a one-crop pattern which exhausted the soil. The sharecrop system, in which the tenant provided his labor for a share of the crop, solved the labor problem that the emancipation of slaves had created. But the method by which farmers financed their operations, the crop-lien system, retarded progress. Under this arrangement farmers pledged their future crops to merchants for credit with which to finance their year's operations. Since in granting such credit the merchant undertook grave risks, he charged high rates of interest and higher prices for goods purchased under the crop lien. Moreover, the system froze patterns of finance and agriculture. Pledged to one merchant, the farmer could not secure credit, and thereby trade, elsewhere. To realize on his investment the merchant often forced the farmer to grow the most profitable cash crop—cotton. For years southern agriculture struggled to free itself from this yoke and to enter upon a more flexible and diversified farming.

Southern agrarians became restless and resentful toward the rising cities, expanding industry, and fresh spirit of the "New South." Suspicious of the urban areas from which pleas for industrialization emanated, frustrated because of their own relative lack of progress, southern agricultural regions often fought legislation intended to foster industrial growth. Led by Tom Watson, the region's most vociferous agrarian rebel, farmers of the South joined the Populist movement to vent their wrath over low cotton prices upon the new urban influences. In the early twentieth century direct descendants of the Populists joined merchants in attacks on the railroads and spearheaded the drive to abolish such aids to industry as the immigration bureaus.

The Response to Industrialism

Underlying these different features of western and southern growth was a common colonial economic position in relationship to the Northeast. Southern and western industry remained largely extractive, producing agricultural goods and industrial raw materials. Compared with New England's 10.7 per cent of workers in extractive industries—agriculture, forestry, animal husbandry, fishing, mining—62 per cent of southern workers held such occupations in 1910. Oil, sulfur, bauxite, copper, lumber, and silver production typified the predominant industrial activity of the South and West.

The meager amount of manufacturing that developed in these sections was confined to the initial processing of crops and resources by low-wage, unskilled labor. Following the colonial economic pattern, most of these products were then fabricated in the East or even abroad. Value added to them by manufacture, usually the largest proportion of the total value of the finished product, went not to the South or West but to the industrial East or Europe. The southern textile industry, for example, specialized in producing yarn and coarse or unfinished cloth, much of which it shipped north for final processing. The South and West semiprocessed much of its wool, beef, lumber, copper, cane sugar, turpentine, rosin, and cottonseed oil, only to forward the products elsewhere for final manufacture. Only rarely did a factory produce finished goods ready for the ultimate consumer; a North Carolina furniture factory, western flour milling, beet-sugar refining, and meat packing were examples of such exceptions.

Southern and western leaders realized that new manufacturing provided the key to regional economic progress; they equally recognized the economic disadvantages under which they labored: meager regional markets, a shortage of skilled labor and technical ability, and insufficient capital. Northeastern economic policies, moreover, tended to augment these difficulties. These policies in part came from a deliberate attempt to restrict the growth of manufacturing in other areas of the country; in part they stemmed from the incidental impact of policies which northeastern industry adopted to stabilize its business.

In order to hold prices firm in the iron and steel industry, for example, northern producers as early as the 1870's established the basing-point system, later known as Pittsburgh Plus: all steel prices throughout the country were quoted as of Pittsburgh plus transportation from that point, irrespective of the distance between buyer and producer. The motive for this policy came from a desire to protect huge investments in steel by stabilizing both output and prices, rather than from a deliberate attempt to retard the growth of the industry elsewhere; but the operation of the system produced such a detrimental effect. When United States Steel in 1907 acquired the Tennessee Coal and Iron Company, owner of the booming Birmingham, Alabama, iron and steel industry, Pittsburgh Plus destroyed the regional advantages of southern producers. If an Alabama steel fabricator purchased steel from Birmingham mills, he paid the Pittsburgh price plus "phantom freight" from Pittsburgh. Such a policy encouraged steel fabricators to locate nearer Pittsburgh to obtain cheaper freight, when without Pittsburgh Plus they would have logically located in the South to secure cheaper steel. Years later an engineering firm reported to United States Steel that the corporation had lost money by not developing more fully its low-cost facilities at Birmingham; the Federal Trade Commission had found that the cost of production at Birmingham was 26 per cent less than at Pittsburgh. The foremost authority on this phase of regional development has concluded: "Basing point pricing in steel has contributed to the South's poverty by curbing the expansion and utilization of its steelmaking facilities and by retarding the growth of steel consuming industries."

Although the railroad aided in developing the South and West, its policies also helped to cement this colonial pattern of economy. Rates on raw materials from the South and West to the Northeast were lower than in the reverse direction, thereby benefiting northeastern consumers of raw materials over their regional competitors. Rates on industrial goods, on the other hand, were lower from the Northeast to the South and West than in the opposite direction. The railroads frequently modified their rates in accordance with the interests of northeastern industry; in 1890, for example, the Pennsylvania Railroad advanced southern iron rates at the request of Pennsylvania ironmen. The roads first established these regional rate patterns by means of pools in the latter quarter of the nineteenth century, and the Interstate Commerce Commission for years permitted them to continue. The differentials enabled railroads to restrict competition from southern and western industry and to reserve markets there for northeastern shippers.

A crucial feature of the colonial economy lay in the inability of the South and West to generate their own surplus capital for investment in productive enterprise. Since they sold raw materials and purchased finished goods, the terms of trade with the Northeast were unfavorable. They were equally unable to draw income into their sections from the processes of trade, transportation, or finance; these were owned by northeasterners who transferred their profits to that section. The South suffered under an additional burden; emancipation of the slaves had destroyed some three billion dollars of capital, and untold amounts more of southern property had been lost during the Civil War.

These sections, therefore, depended for their development upon external sources of funds. After the depression of 1873 northern and British capital flowed into railroads, mines, financial houses, distribution facilities, and industrial enterprise. For those who wished to invest, however, the possibilities of northeastern enterprise seemed far more profitable. Mining attracted sufficient capital; but investors were far more dubious about agriculture, in which at times they had lost heavily. The severe winter of 1887–88 on the western range wiped out extensive British investments in the cattle industry. Easterners who had provided funds for western irrigation enterprise suffered severely in the depression in the late eighties and early nineties and were reluctant to provide funds for a similar purpose for well over a decade. The investments which did materialize only intensified the disadvantageous position of these sections. For with "foreign" capital came "foreign" control. The new businessmen, agents and retainers of northern industry, returned their profits to stockholders who lived outside the West or South.

THE POLITICS OF COLONIALISM

The South and the West increasingly blamed their troubles on the Northeast. To curb the "unfair" advantages of that section and to enlarge their own opportunities for economic growth, these underdeveloped areas demanded public action on a wide front. Both sections, for example, sought from the federal government agricultural capital which private bankers refused to lend at the rates they desired. A Rural Credits Act in 1916 established the Federal Farm Land Bank system which provided mortgage loans at longer terms and lower interest rates than commercial bankers offered. The South demanded commodity loans as well. In the early 1890's the Farmers' Alliance popularized a plan that provided for federal subtreasuries throughout the agricultural area to serve as depositories for crops. On the security of these commodities the federal government would grant loans and thereby enable the cotton farmer to hold his crop from the market until he could secure a more advantageous price. Although the South obtained federal legislation in 1916 which established warehousing standards for private commodity loans, it did not secure public commodity loans until the 1930's.

For development capital the South and West hoped to secure an increasing share of federal public works expenditures. A northeastern-dominated Congress, so argued those sections, discriminated against their regions in federal appropriations; it refused to expand the scope of public works beyond the traditional naval construction and rivers and harbors development to include projects more beneficial to other sections of the country. When private funds for irrigation declined early in the 1890's, the West demanded federal irrigation financing. In 1894, in the Carey Act, Congress granted public lands to western states which they in turn could sell to promote irrigation. But little development took place under this law. Western leaders, therefore, shifted their tactics to demand outright appropriations through the rivers and harbors fund. Rebuffed here, the West in 1902 obtained the Newlands Irrigation Act, in which the proceeds from the sale of public lands, set aside in a special Reclamation Fund, provided the capital to finance development. The Newlands Act passed only over bitter opposition from eastern congressmen who argued that it would create unfair western competition with eastern farmers.

The South also sought more of the federal largess. The Mississippi River had long received rivers and harbors funds largely because the Northeast needed the votes of the lower Valley to pass its bills. This aid, however, was confined to navigation and did not meet the need for funds to drain the rich Mississippi Delta. Moreover, private drainage had already intensified the danger of recurring Mississippi floods; the South demanded more federal funds for flood control. For many years the Northeast warded off both these pleas, but in the field of flood control it finally gave way. First allowing small flood-control appropriations in rivers and harbors bills under the guise of aid to navigation, Congress in 1917 finally passed a full-fledged Mississippi River flood-control measure.

The financial problems of the South and West played an important part in framing the Federal Reserve Act of 1913, which provided for a more flexible currency and for a method to mobilize bank reserves throughout the nation in periods of crisis. The National Monetary Commission, established in 1907 and headed by Senator Nelson Aldrich of Rhode Island, had recommended a single national banking system as in England, in which the nation's leading banks would play the dominant role. Convinced that just such control prevented them from securing both long- and short-term credit, the South and the West modified the bill to provide for federal influence in Federal Reserve policies. Moreover, twelve regional banks replaced the one central bank; the underdeveloped sections felt that banks in their own areas would respond far more readily to their needs than would a central organization undoubtedly to be located in New York City.

Sectional politics in the Progressive Era often took the form of an economic and political revolt against the railroads. The impetus for this reaction lay not alone in the organizational revolution among shippers but involved also a regional revulsion against several decades of railroad leadership in economic development. The rate policies of railroads, it was argued, retarded regional industrial growth. Merchants and shippers who complained of adverse rate patterns could marshal in their favor a regional conviction that the railroads in their areas were in league with northeastern business. Moreover, the railroads had become dominant in the politics of many southern and western states and thereby had kept state policies in line with their views of regional growth. The revolt against the railroads, therefore, became political as well as economic. The "progressive" political factions of such governors as Albert Cummins in Iowa, Robert La Follette in Wisconsin, Braxton Bragg Comer in Alabama, and Hoke Smith in Georgia rallied the sentiment of merchants and others concerned with regional economic problems to take political action to overthrow the railroad "machines." State railroad regulation and measures to outlaw free passes for legislators became major instruments whereby "progressives" hoped to curtail the influence of railroads in their region.

The issue of tariff duties on imports to protect American producers from foreign competition aroused especially bitter sectional controversy. The heavily industrialized Northeast sought high rates on its manufactures and low duties on its raw materials; the non-industrialized areas of the West and South demanded the reverse, tariffs on their agricultural and raw-material products but free trade in food and supplies which they purchased. These sections argued that the industrial tariff drained needed funds from their regions by forcing them to buy on a protected market at higher prices while they sold their major farm products on an unprotected world market at lower prices. Moreover, those industries and commodity groups which looked to prosperity through expanded foreign markets—iron and steel, farm equipment, wheat and cotton, for example—approved reciprocal trade agreements in which foreign countries would open their markets to more American goods if the United States, in turn, would lower its barriers to foreign-made products.

Although the tariff debate often centered around the interest of consumers, who bore the brunt of the duties in the form of higher prices, the alignment of forces depended more on the interests of producers. If an important industry sought protection, its demands would weigh heavily with the legislator from its district. A congressman could afford to support the consumer point of view only if among his constituents no industrialist demanded aid. Debate on the tariff in terms of principle, therefore, and detailed arguments about the difference in cost of production at home and abroad merely obscured the more basic dissensions among the producers of various sections. For the most part the conflict lay between industrial and agricultural areas; but upon this theme there were important variations.

The bloc which passed the Morrill Act of 1861, the first significant protective tariff of the modern industrial era, originated as a combination of New England textile and Middle Atlantic iron and steel interests. Because it had little to protect, the agricultural Old Northwest looked upon this legislation as eastern industrial robbery of western agrarian consumers; but until the South, where a similar sentiment prevailed, returned fully to the Union in 1877, this opposition stormed in vain. The tariff bloc soon added strength to meet this new threat; it invaded the Old Northwest itself, first attracting Ohio and Michigan by protecting their rapidly growing iron, steel, copper, lumber, and wool production, and later bringing Illinois and finally Indiana and Wisconsin into the fold. By the end of the 1880's the entire area voted predominantly for high tariffs. As rapidly as territories of the Far West became states, they too were enticed into the alliance through duties on grain, flax, wool, hides, and beet sugar; solidly affirmed in the McKinley Act of 1890 and the Dingley Act of 1897, the loyalty of the Mountain region and Far West to a high tariff persisted through the years to come.

Laws passed by the tariff bloc posed headaches for New England industry, which now faced higher prices for important raw materials, wool and hides, fuel, and iron and steel. Though leaders of that section refused to consider reducing tariffs on products they manufactured, in the 1880's they began a campaign to abolish duties on raw materials. The Democrats in 1887 seized upon this discontent to increase their strength in Republican New England; in 1888 they pitched their presidential campaign on the tariff issue. Although thwarted at that time, the New England free raw-material movement continued; as Democratic strength grew in such states as Massachusetts during the first decade of the twentieth century, even Republicans took up the cry. President Taft (1857–1930) responded to this demand; in the struggle to enact the Payne-Aldrich Tariff of 1909 he refused to withdraw his insistence on free hides. Two years later he pushed through Congress the Canadian Reciprocity Treaty. While granting few concessions on manufactures, the treaty lowered United States duties on raw materials from Canada, a provision highly pleasing to American manufacturers.

The western Middle West and the South became the most persistent critics of the rising industrial tariff. Predominantly agricultural, neither area contained important industries to protect; in both regions, however, there were significant exceptions. The South, for example, with expanding coal and iron production, opposed New England's demand for free raw materials; in the Wilson-Gorman Act of 1894 votes from the South helped to thwart that movement. The western Middle West, on the other hand, rose quickly to defend its beet-sugar, linseed-oil, and other agricultural processing industries. Yet, since the bulk of protected manufactures were in the Northeast, the predominant viewpoint of other sections reflected the typical agrarian reaction to the industrial tariff. Governor Albert Cummins of Iowa spearheaded a midwestern tariff revolt in the first decade of the twentieth century. His "Iowa idea," the view that no tariff which fostered a trust should be permitted, served as the major ideological vehicle for the grain-belt demand for lower duties.

In 1909 a small band of midwestern senators, Insurgents in the Republican party, launched a prolonged and detailed attack on the highly protective Payne-Aldrich bill. These men did not hold low-tariff principles, nor were they fighting the battles of urban consumers. Representing one of the few areas of the country for which the Payne-Aldrich bill provided no crumbs, they could afford to take the lead in demanding a lower industrial tariff. Their struggle, which failed, played a far greater role in creating a split within the Republican party than in furthering the cause of tariff reform. Moreover, their sectional interests clearly emerged when President Taft, partly to embarrass the Insurgents' low-duty professions, pushed through the Senate the Canadian Reciprocity Treaty in 1911. The midwesterners were furious that the treaty provided for free import of competing grain and cattle from Canada. In return they unsuccessfully sought to attach to the reciprocity measure amendments providing for their kind of tariff reform, lower duties on goods which farmers purchased. When Congress later passed these amendments separately as the Farmers' Free List tariff bill, Taft vetoed them on the ground that they were not "scientifically" constructed.

The new Democratic administration of Woodrow Wilson in 1913 brought about the first major tariff reduction since the Civil War. The Underwood-Simmons Act of that year lowered duties on more than nine hundred items and placed important articles such as iron, steel, agricultural machinery, clothing, food, and shoes on the free list. Fashioned under the influence of southern Democratic leaders, the bill fulfilled the demands of the agrarian consumer. Yet for these gains southern and western producers paid their price; Wilson forced into the bill provisions for free sugar and free wool. The

The Response to Industrialism

Underwood-Simmons Act hardly took effect; for World War I began shortly after it passed, and after the war the Republicans continued to raise duties to even higher levels.

The tariff issue involved questions of finance as well as protection for local enterprise. Prior to the income tax the tariff constituted the largest single source of federal revenue; timing of tariff debates, therefore, depended as much on the condition of the federal treasury as on changing sectional economic interests. After the Civil War an increasing surplus and steady reduction of the federal debt weakened one of the protectionists' strongest arguments, that the tariff brought in needed revenue. To solve this problem the tariff bloc in the 1880's lowered duties on tea and coffee, the most prolific revenue producers, and increased federal expenditures. Low-tariff advocates, on the other hand, realizing full well that such a program would justify higher duties, fought to raise the rates on tea and coffee to bring in more revenue.

The politics of federal taxation became as bitter and as sectional as the politics of protection. The South and the West especially sought means other than the tariff to raise needed revenue. Since their sections consumed protected items, southerners and westerners argued, the tariff was actually a tax on them. Convinced that the protected industries themselves did not contribute their share to the federal treasury, leaders of the South and West advocated an income tax to equalize the federal revenue burden. Under pressure from these sections, for example, Congress retained the Civil War income tax until 1872. The income tax was especially popular among owners of real property, who felt that newer forms of wealth represented by paper values rather than by tangible goods too often escaped their just share of taxation. The agrarian property-holders of the South and West had traditionally held such views; in the

Populist-Progressive Era they bore the brunt of the fight for an income-tax law.

Immediately after the depression of 1893, when federal revenue declined drastically, the South and the West attached to the Wilson-Gorman tariff of 1894 a federal tax of 2 per cent on incomes over $4,000. The following year, however, the Supreme Court in *Pollock* v. *Farmers' Loan and Trust Company* declared this law unconstitutional. The Court's decision prompted bitter hostility. But not until the Payne-Aldrich tariff came up in 1909 did the South and the West again obtain an opportunity to enact an income tax. By this time increasing federal expenditures had created a need for new sources of revenue. Fear that the Court would again declare such a tax unconstitutional prompted Congress to seek other methods of raising funds; the Payne-Aldrich bill provided for a corporation tax. Yet the same Congress approved an income-tax amendment which the states ratified early in 1913 as the Sixteenth Amendment. That same year in the Underwood-Simmons Act, Congress approved a measure by Representative Cordell Hull (1871–1955) of Tennessee that provided for the first permanent income-tax law in the United States. Although Insurgent Republicans did not obtain as steeply graduated rates as they desired, this act marked the beginnings of what eventually became the primary source of federal revenue.

Sectional antagonism toward the Northeast received its fullest expression in the attack on "trusts" and the demand for legislation to control them. Historians have not yet discovered which specific economic groups sought antitrust laws. However, the first state antitrust laws came primarily in the South and West, and those regions led both in criticism of the trusts and in demands for legislation to curb them. It seems likely that antitrust sentiment in these areas did not stem from the specific economic effects of mergers on southern and western entrepreneurs so much as it symbolized the subordinate economic position of their regions and the frustrated hopes for more rapid growth. This is not to say that mergers had no adverse effect on regional economic activities but merely to point out that regional antitrust sentiment was stronger than presently known specific economic grievances can explain.

Although Congress passed the original federal antitrust law, the Sherman Act, in 1890, antitrust agitation prior to 1897 had not been well organized or particularly strong. After that time, however, antitrust sentiment increased rapidly and brought the issue into vigorous public debate during the first years of the twentieth century. The timing of this increased activity stemmed from the increasing number of mergers themselves and undoubtedly from the impact of these mergers on various sectors of the economy. In response to this agitation the United States Industrial Commission undertook an investigation of trusts in 1900, and bills appeared in Congress to deal more effectively with them. A Bureau of Corporations was established in the new Department of Commerce and Labor in 1903, with power to investigate and publicize but not to enforce.

During the same years President Theodore Roosevelt undertook to apply the Sherman Act against a number of large corporations. Prior to this time the Supreme Court had invoked the Sherman Act effectively against loose combinations, agreements among competitors to fix prices, allocate production, or otherwise restrain trade. But it had refused to proceed against tight combinations, outright mergers or holding companies which controlled a large percentage of production in their fields. In the E. C. Knight case in 1895, for example, the Court argued that although the American Sugar Refining Company controlled 98 per cent of the refining capacity of the country, it did not constitute a conspiracy to restrain trade under the Sherman Act. That act, the Court maintained, applied not to production but to commerce, and sugar refining was not commerce. Since the Court did not move against the larger combinations, the public felt erroneously that the Sherman Act lay dormant. The Roosevelt administration, however, did move against the new corporate giants and persuaded the Court to apply the act in the case of such tight combinations as the Northern Securities Company (a railroad combination), the Standard Oil Company, and the American Tobacco Company.

These proceedings raised the question as to how action could be taken to restrain "monopoly" without destroying the possible efficiencies of combination. From the West came proposals to break up trusts into small units; both William Jennings Bryan and Senator La Follette argued that no corporation should be permitted to own more than a given share of the assets or manufacture more than a given proportion of the production of all firms in its field. Roosevelt, who labeled La Follette a "rural Tory" because of these views, argued that corporations should not be restricted or broken up but should be supervised by the federal government. The supervisory agency should enforce publicity of operations and restrict such activity as outright dishonesty and stock-watering, according to Roosevelt, and this point of view prevailed in new antitrust legislation in 1914. The Clayton Act of that year spelled out more precisely the practices that constituted restraints of trade, and a companion measure established a supervisory Federal Trade Commission which was to secure and publicize factual information, investigate complaints, and initiate proceedings against violators of the law.

VII. The Politics of Adjustment

To cushion the impact of industrialism, the people of the United States invariably sought assistance from government. Americans had rarely considered their government to be neutral; they believed that it should stand by as a powerful instrument of positive support when needed. As earlier they had called upon public agencies to finance railroad construction, for example, they now looked to the same source to control railroad rates and to protect them from other adverse effects of industrialism. But those in positions of political power rebuffed attempts to obtain access to government for these new objectives. The struggle over influence in the decision-making process constituted a major feature of the Progressive Era; it produced conflicts between and within the political parties, led to the rapid growth of new extra-party techniques through which measures rejected by parties could receive support, and precipitated a re-evaluation of the role of the Supreme Court in the American political system.

THE POLITICAL IDEOLOGY OF ADJUSTMENT

To the great majority of Americans in the Progressive Era the nation's problems could be reduced to a contest for power between the "interests" and the "people." The country's ills stemmed from monopoly, the increasing concentration of business which was choking off opportunity in every field of economic, social, and political life. Strike down monopoly by means of governmental regulation of business, and opportunity could be restored. But the close alliance between the business corporation and the politician prevented passage of such legislation. Behind every resistance to change, the American people found a corporation. Did not Lincoln Steffens and other writers reveal clearly that business financed both political parties, dictated the choice of candidates, and lobbied to choke off bills hostile to corporations? Political reform, therefore, must precede legislation; once the "people" could express their views unhampered by corporate influence, they could solve their problems.

These popular beliefs did not stem solely from the factual revelations of the behavior of corporations. They arose also because vast changes caused by impersonal industrial forces could easily be attributed to the personal behavior of businessmen. Farmers, workers, and small businessmen blamed large corporations for those limitations on economic opportunity which were inherent in the new technology and the price-and-market system. City dwellers attributed the urban problems which arose from the birth pangs of modern metropolitan life to the "public be damned" attitude of business. To such writers as Lincoln Steffens, for example, the power of city bosses depended on their corrupt relationships with businessmen and not on the crucial role that machine leaders played in the immigrant's life. Consumers ascribed the rising cost of living to monopolies. And native Americans blamed the businessman for encouraging immigration and thereby undermining American institutions. This is not to say that the newness and the behavior of corporate monsters themselves did not frighten Americans; they did.

The Response to Industrialism

But hostility toward corporations resulted even more from the fact that they served as convenient scapegoats; they were held personally responsible for conditions which in fact were almost inevitable features of industrial change.

Those who agreed that corporations were responsible for all that was wrong with American society often pursued vastly different aims. They faced a common enemy, corporate business; they all sought reforms through state and federal legislation; they agreed on the necessity of electoral changes. But beyond this point they worked for different, and frequently contradictory, objectives. Humanitarians and labor leaders, for example, maintained a mutual suspicion; in railroad regulation, railroad labor and shippers came to blows, the workers demanding rate increases and the shippers opposing them; farmers, who distrusted all things urban, did not look with favor upon the demands of municipal reformers. These different groups joined to make change possible, but they differed widely on what precise changes should be made. They agreed on the means of action but not on the ends. If we concentrate on the ideology and methods of reform in the early twentieth century, we obtain the false picture of a revolt against a common enemy for a common purpose. But by probing deeper to discover the positive goals of each group, we find vastly different, often conflicting, aims. The only unifying factor among these positive goals is that each group was trying to cope with changes brought about by industrialism.

The political ideology of the Populist-Progressive Era, moreover, did not accurately describe the nature either of the reform movements of the time or of their opposition. The "people" proved to be especially difficult to define. Agricultural shippers, for example, demanded a "people's counsel" as an adjunct to the Interstate Commerce Commission to represent the "people's" case before that body. But who were the people? The shippers? Consumers and railroad labor might not consider such a counsel a "people's counsel." Almost every movement of the Progressive Era subscribed to the concept of the "people" and believed that its demands sprang from them. But the "people," in fact, often opposed reforms. Immigrant votes enabled urban machines to defeat municipal reforms; just as often farmers stifled change. Support for change, therefore, stemmed from a more complex source than the "people," and opposition to it came from a wider variety of groups than the corporation.

PARTY POLITICS

The two decades of economic expansion between 1874 and 1894 witnessed a party politics that reflected the spirit of the age: reckless, competitive, blustering, and devoted to the nation's rapid material growth. Neither party dominated the federal government for any length of time. Although the Democrats won a majority of the presidential popular vote in four of the five elections between 1876 and 1892 and lost the election of 1880 by only 7,000 votes, they failed in 1876 and again in 1888 to secure a majority in the electoral college. Although the Democrats controlled the House of Representatives in eight of the ten Congresses between 1874 and 1894, the Senate went Republican seven times. These twenty years of stalemate produced no sustained working majorities; only twice, the Republicans in the 1889–91 Congress and the Democrats in the 1893–95 session, did a single party control presidency and Congress. Small wonder that these were decades of political confusion.

In 1894 the Republican party broke this political stalemate when it swept the congressional election to inaugurate a sixteen-year GOP reign in the national legislature. McKinley's 1896 victory began an equally long Republican stay in the White House; Theo-

The Response to Industrialism

dore Roosevelt followed McKinley, after the latter's assassination in 1901, secured re-election in 1904, and gave way to William Howard Taft in 1909. In Congress the party developed a tightly knit, highly effective organization in both House and Senate, which enabled it to direct the course of legislation for many years. In the House the all-powerful Speaker exercised authority to institute rules of procedure and to appoint committees. Here a small core of Republicans dominated proceedings. They were led by Speaker "Uncle Joe" Cannon (1836–1926), a crusty old watchdog over the federal treasury who opposed every social critic and reformer with the abrupt quip, "This country is a hell of a success. . . ." In the Senate an inner circle of four Republican senators ruled with as firm a hand and as great hostility for change as marked the House leadership. Between 1894 and 1910 the Republican party controlled the federal government to a degree rarely known in American political history.

Against this Republican leadership those who wished new legislation to tackle problems created by industrialism struggled for recognition. Republican leaders did not look with favor when reformers demanded railroad regulation, waterways expansion, tariff tampering, social welfare legislation, or conservation; in 1907 "Uncle Joe" personally fought off an immigrant literacy test. To counteract these requests, the party leaders drew the reins even tighter. They appointed to key committees members who they knew were opposed to reforms and upon whom they could rely to nip such measures in the bud; they exercised an especially watchful eye on appropriations that might expand reform activities.

Theodore Roosevelt used his influence to break down this resistance to change. Although McKinley hesitated to take action that might alienate congressional leaders, Roosevelt, with a flair for the dramatic and a keen understanding of changing grass-roots political sentiment, struck out more boldly. The new President took up causes dear to the West to which he had been politically attached for some time. Over the vigorous opposition of House Republican leaders, in 1902 he successfully promoted the Newlands Irrigation Act. In 1905–6, by threatening to take up the tariff issue, he artfully committed the same politicians to a more effective interstate commerce law, ardently desired by the West. In 1902 he initiated the Northern Securities case, the first major successful prosecution of a "tight combination" under the Sherman Antitrust Act. To force a reluctant Congress to approve administration-sponsored conservation measures, Roosevelt in 1908 called a widely publicized Governors' Conference at Washington, ostensibly to promote conservation education, but politically designed to arouse public opinion.

Yet Roosevelt alone could not force the hand of the congressional leaders. Success came to him most quickly when he received support from a strategic bloc within the Republican party that was none too happy with the views of the party's congressional leaders. A group of senators from the Mountain region and Far West gave special trouble. In 1890 the eastern wing of the party had been forced to support the Sherman Silver Purchase Act and a tariff on western farm products in return for western votes for a higher tariff on eastern industrial goods. In 1902 western senators obtained the Newlands Act only after they had filibustered to death an eastern-sponsored rivers and harbors bill and had forced Republican leaders to meet their terms or face similar action in the future. Roosevelt's skilful handling of the Hepburn Act to strengthen the Interstate Commerce Commission, on the other hand, depended largely on the strong western and southern sentiment in Congress for railroad regulation.

Other movements received far less support from crucial factions in Congress and therefore did not as readily achieve their aims.

The Response to Industrialism

Even Roosevelt either rebuffed them or refused to champion their cause. Urban humanitarians, such as those in the women's clubs, though ardent and widely heard through the magazines and newspapers, were numerically weak. Few city politicians heeded their voice, and even Roosevelt turned a cold shoulder to them until he needed their support in 1912. Organized labor, rebuffed by the Republicans, found a more receptive audience in Democratic ranks. Republican leaders of a reinvigorated, or "progressive," section of the party in the Middle West constituted a far more troublesome minority. Coming to power in their own states on the strength of an antirailroad movement, they moved on to Washington to demand more drastic railroad regulation, substantial tariff reform, and other sectional economic measures; neither Congress nor Roosevelt would fully support their program. In 1904, when the duly elected Robert La Follette "progressive" delegates from Wisconsin appeared at the Republican National Convention, they were refused seats; the convention admitted a rebel "stalwart" faction instead. In 1908 the convention turned down decisively a Wisconsin-sponsored platform that would have committed the party to many of the midwestern-sponsored reforms.

By 1909 these midwestern Insurgents comprised a sizable bloc of opposition within the Republican party. Led by a group of senators, La Follette of Wisconsin, Cummins and Dolliver of Iowa, Clapp and Nelson of Minnesota, and Bristow of Kansas, the rebels formed a well-organized challenge to the party leadership. They took their stand first on the Payne-Aldrich Tariff of 1909; while careful not to disturb protection for midwestern products, for three months they fought, unsuccessfully, to lower schedules on industrial goods that their section purchased. In the House the Insurgents' major victory was to curb the rules-making power of Speaker

The Politics of Adjustment

Cannon. When Taft opposed them on the tariff, the midwesterners sought every opportunity to embarrass the administration. For example, in the winter of 1909–10 they took up the Pinchot-Ballinger controversy, involving a dispute over changes which Taft had made in Roosevelt's conservation policy, but which easily became diverted into a charge of dishonesty on the part of Taft's Secretary of the Interior, Richard A. Ballinger, in handling Alaskan coal lands. When the President supported his Secretary in this controversy, the Insurgents relentlessly accused Taft of complicity in a dishonest act.

Prior to 1909 Theodore Roosevelt had been able to placate or, co-operating fully with the party leaders, to crush an incipient Insurgency. But Taft, now facing a more powerful and determined revolt, failed to prevent an open break between the Old Guard and their opponents; it is doubtful if Roosevelt could have mediated more successfully. Once faced with revolt, Taft and the Old Guard tried to defeat their opponents, first with their patronage power and then by entering the 1910 midwestern primaries against them. Badly defeated here, the administration held out the olive branch to promote a united front against the Democrats in 1912; for example, two men closely associated with the Insurgents found posts in the Taft cabinet in the spring of 1911. But the midwestern leaders failed to respond; their opposition had gone too far. By now they were supported by almost every group in the country which the Republican leadership had thwarted over the past decade. Although these groups found little common ground, as we have seen, they readily joined in attacking the administration's policies. They co-operated with the Insurgent leaders to form the National Progressive Republican League, designed to defeat Taft's bid for renomination in 1912.

The rebels soon fell to quarreling over who would lead them in that campaign year, Senator Robert La Follette or Theodore Roosevelt. This was no mere difference in personalities. For by 1912 Roosevelt seemed to voice particularly the demands arising from urban and humanitarian reform, while La Follette was more closely associated with sectional economic aspirations and the strivings of organized labor, agriculture, and shippers. La Follette spearheaded the attack on Taft at first, but when Roosevelt returned from his African game hunt, his admirers finally persuaded him to run. At the 1912 Republican convention, although Roosevelt received most of the anti-Taft votes, President Taft, by his control of the party machinery, easily won renomination. Charging fraud, the Roosevelt adherents organized their own Progressive party, nominated the ex-President as their candidate, and jumped into the campaign of 1912. Their major impact was to split Republican support, permitting the Democrat, Woodrow Wilson, to win the presidency with only 42 per cent of the popular vote.

The Progressive party quickly declined. Its extremely weak showing in 1914 gubernatorial and senatorial contests persuaded most of the rebels to seek readmission to the Republican party; although diehards renominated Roosevelt on a Progressive ticket in 1916, he refused to run. For their failure, Progressives accused each other. Rabid antitrust segments of the party attributed it to their fairy godfathers, George Perkins of J. P. Morgan and Company and Frank Munsey of *Munsey's* magazine, whose financial support and consequent prominence hardly helped to persuade voters that the party fought monopolies. These leaders, on the other hand, blamed the "radical" faction, the "lunatic fringe" as Roosevelt himself called it. But the major cause lay in the fact that the Progressive party failed to develop strong organizational support at the grass roots. Its following testified to Roosevelt's personal popularity and to vigorous assent for his ceremonial warfare against industrial evil; but this same following failed to give state candidates more than pitifully weak support even in 1912. Few popular, organized grass-roots demands found a voice through the Progressive party.

Soon after the election of 1904 Republican success at the polls began to wane. Beginning in the election of 1906, Democratic strength as reflected by its control of seats in the House of Representatives grew steadily each two-year interval, finally reaching a peak in 1912. By 1910 the party captured control of the House and won governorships in New York, New Jersey, Ohio, and Indiana, as well as in Maine and Oregon. The center of this upsurge lay in a belt of states from New York and New Jersey on the east to Illinois on the west. But its cause is not entirely clear. The popular Insurgent attack on Taft provides a partial explanation for increased Democratic strength in 1910 but does not explain the earlier beginning of the Democratic upswing or its concentration in a particular section. It also appears that rural-sponsored laws prohibiting the use of alcoholic beverages persuaded some industrial cities to go Democratic; in New Jersey, for example, prohibition played an important role in enabling north Jersey urban Democrats to seize control of the reform movement from "progressive" Republicans. The roots of the Democratic revival remain an enigma.

The congressional victories of 1910 set off a scramble for the Democratic presidential nomination two years later; the Republican split, virtually assuring a Democratic victory, intensified the contest in the Democratic party convention in 1912. Although Speaker of the House Champ Clark (1850–1921) of Missouri held a majority of the convention's votes, he did not receive the required two-thirds. Instead, the nomination went to a relative newcomer in politics, Governor Woodrow Wilson of New Jersey. Wilson was a brilliant and popular speaker, a man of firm moral convictions, who strongly believed that a chief executive should lead rather than follow Congress. He had given up the practice of law at an early age to become a college professor, and in 1902 he was selected president of Princeton University. Elected governor of New Jersey in 1910, Wilson had earned an enviable reputation by championing progressive measures; he gained special prominence when he forced the Democratic legislators, against their wishes, to abide by a popular advisory vote in selecting a United States senator. While Taft and Roosevelt vied to smear each other's character in the ensuing campaign, Wilson easily loped to victory.

The new President, however, did not prove to be the reforming executive which such urban Democratic mayors as Tom Johnson of Cleveland and John Purroy Mitchel of New York City had hoped. Southern Democrats, who had contributed much to Wilson's nomination, and who lacked enthusiasm for urban-oriented reform, reinforced the cautious views of the President. The major legislation of the first Wilson administration—the Underwood Tariff, the Federal Reserve Act, and the Clayton Antitrust Act—followed closely southern sectional interest in lower tariffs and southern hostility toward eastern bankers and industry. Equal significance lay in the proposed bills of which Wilson disapproved. He rejected a measure to institute a federal farm-mortgage credit system on the grounds that it anticipated a radically new function for the federal government; for similar reasons he turned down child labor legislation. To Wilson the primary function of government was to destroy roadblocks to opportunity, not to provide positive services for the American people.

Facing the election of 1916, however, Wilson approved some of these same reforms. Since the administration could not count on another Republican family fight to hand it victory, it sought added votes by securing in 1916 a farm-mortgage credit act, the Keating-Owen Child Labor Act, the Adamson Act, which granted railway operating employees the eight-hour day, and a federal workmen's compensation measure. Despite these lures, Wilson barely squeaked past his Republican opponent, Charles Evans Hughes (1862–1948); the deciding vote from California was not known for several days after the election. The Democratic party's congressional power declined from its earlier comfortable margin to a bare working majority. This was only the beginning of a precipitate decrease in strength which completed the Democratic cycle of growth and decline; as voters reacted from the administration's wartime policies, Democratic fortunes slid further in 1918 and hit rock bottom in the overwhelming Republican victory of 1920.

The Progressive Era witnessed the rise of the Socialist party as the major third party of the time. Organized in 1901 from a number of former factions, the Socialist party of America doubled its membership between 1904 and 1908 and within the next four years tripled its numbers to reach a peak of 117,984 in 1912. In that year Eugene Debs (1855–1926), the Socialist candidate for President, polled 897,000 votes, 6 per cent of the total popular vote cast and the greatest percentage strength in the party's history. Debs, radical but not doctrinaire, attracted a sympathetic following far greater in number than the Socialists themselves. Five times between 1900 and 1920 he ran for the presidency as the party's standard-bearer, and in his last attempt in 1920, while in federal prison for violating the sedition provisions of the Espionage Act, he polled over 900,000 votes.

The Socialists comprised a wide variety of groups and individuals: midwestern farmers of Populist tradition—the party was strongest in Oklahoma; industrial workers in especially desperate circumstances, such as western miners whose unionization efforts frequently met defeat; German and Jewish immigrants for whom socialism constituted more of an attempt to preserve a cultural identity than a radical plan of action; and a great number of profes-

The Response to Industrialism

sionals, lawyers, doctors, and ministers, for whom the Socialist party continued the spirit of Bellamy Nationalism to supplant American materialistic competition with a truly co-operative commonwealth. Yet these groups possessed a unifying element; their membership in the party revealed a common feeling of alienation from American society, a belief that society was unresponsive to their values and goals. Their common ground was dissent; a joint socialistic philosophy represented less a blueprint which would have satisfied all than a position from which they could register a collective protest against the existing order.

THE ATTACK ON PARTY POLITICS

In the Progressive Era the Republican and Democratic parties constituted the major avenues of political expression in the United States. Yet, many groups did not find these organizations responsive to their interests. Consequently, they demanded important modifications in the established forms of political expression and promoted new extra-party political techniques.

Partisan politics hampered those groups which arose in industry, labor, and agriculture. Party leaders were concerned primarily with the welfare of their organizations and only incidentally cared to champion measures advocated by others. Where the party stressed compromise of many conflicting interests behind a platform that alienated the fewest, the economic organization feared that compromise would limit its action and dissipate its resources in the support of measures in which it had no direct interest. Governmental agencies, moreover, responded far more readily to the clear-cut aims of non-partisan groups than to the diffuse interests of political parties. Finally, for the politician the party was an end in itself, but for leaders in industry, labor, and agriculture, political action became a means to an end, an instrument to promote their economic interests. After flirting with political parties in the decades after the Civil War, these organizations soon discovered fundamental conflicts in objectives; consequently they sought to free themselves from the limitations of partisan activity. Some solved the problem by completely dominating party action; others, which could not use this method, sought to influence politicians through "pressure groups." But in each case they experimented with thoroughly non-partisan techniques, which would submerge party activity beneath the practice of economic politics.

Industrial leaders pioneered in the struggle of economic groups to emancipate themselves from partisanship. Their technique was to dominate party activity to render it subservient to their wishes. In the post–Civil War years industry and politicians had maintained a mutually helpful alliance, but increasingly corporation leaders found themselves subject to demands for greater financial contributions and threatened with "spite" bills, which politicians proposed primarily to secure favors for not passing them. To control party activity in their interest, corporation leaders in the late 1880's began to participate more actively in the party machinery itself, often as party managers, but more frequently as United States senators in their respective states. To be free from interparty bickering, they sought to control both Republicans and Democrats. Soon known as the "Millionaires' Club," the Senate came to be representative of different economic groups rather than of the states; there were lumber senators, silver senators, and many others. Party leaders functioned now as servants of the new business politicians rather than as masters. Corporate influence in party machinery reached its peak when a Cleveland traction and steel magnate, Mark Hanna (1837–1904), who twice before had failed to realize his ambition of becoming a President-maker, won the Republican presidential nomination in 1896 for his candidate, William McKinley, and rose to the position of Republican national chairman. McKinley, a colorless and weak executive, played his role for Hanna well until his untimely death at the hands of an assassin in 1901.

Other economic groups, with financial resources far less than those of industry, could not dominate the political process; yet they equally sought to be free from the limitations of partisan activity. The trade union, the farm co-operative, and the merchant association provided the economic strength upon which business politics was based. Organized labor and farmers, after their unfortunate experience with partisan activity in the eighties and nineties, shunned participation in third parties; instead they mastered the technique of non-partisan "pressure-group" action. They formed blocs of interest groups in Congress—the labor bloc, fifteen strong in the House in 1910, and the farm bloc, organized first in 1921— which were thoroughly non-partisan and committed to the welfare of the occupational group whose interest they reflected. Such political alignments increasingly subordinated the party process to non-party organizations that arose because of the inability of the party to give voice clearly to their views. Group representation before legislative bodies, in fact, broadened the avenues of political expression beyond that which the political party could provide.

All those whose demands had been thwarted by partisan politics joined to secure widespread innovations in electoral machinery to render representative government more responsive to their interests. This flurry of political reform in the Progressive Era arose not from belief in a deeply held principle but from the actual experience that parties, as then constituted, resisted change. Political reform was an instrument of political warfare. When it was to their advantage to do so, those who demanded reform often later refused to utilize the very techniques they had earlier championed. In Iowa, for example, the "progressive" Republicans obtained a law in 1907 which provided that candidates be selected by popular vote in a primary election. Yet, one year later, "progressive" leaders preferred to select their nominee for the Senate through the state legislative caucus rather than through a primary, because they controlled the party's contingent in the legislature and feared that their candidate might lose in a popular vote. From that time on, conservative Republicans, since they did not control the state party's machinery, became the champions of the primary in Iowa while the Progressives even asked that it be abolished. Reformers demanded electoral changes not because they believed in certain political principles but because they hoped that new techniques in politics would enable them to overcome their opposition. In the Progressive Era political reform was almost the sole common ground upon which differing groups could unite. The National Progressive Republican League, whose major unifying force consisted of anti-Taft sentiment, confined its program largely to electoral reform; it is doubtful if the League could have achieved similar unanimity on more positive substantive issues.

Electoral changes appeared in rapid-fire order. The secret Australian ballot, which enabled the voter to cast his ballot in private, insured his independence from "machine" pressures at the polls. Direct primaries removed the nomination of party candidates from a convention controlled by party workers and placed it in the hands of the voters. Senatorial elections, formerly the province of state legislators who seemed distressingly susceptible to outside influences, came under popular control in the Seventeenth Amendment, adopted in 1913. The initiative, referendum, and recall, which involved legislation by direct popular will, became far more controversial. This direct legislation, established widely first in the state of Oregon and therefore known as the "Oregon system," was popularized throughout the country by its Oregon champion, William S. U'Ren.

The Response to Industrialism

Cities and states adopted portions of the "Oregon system" but usually not its full range of proposals.

Agitation for woman suffrage also increased rapidly during the Progressive Era. Although women played an active role in the humanitarian and prohibition movements, their political influence remained restricted by their inability to vote. For decades a small group of women had labored to extend the suffrage to their sex, but without enthusiastic support from either male legislators or from the majority of politically apathetic women. As women increasingly participated in public affairs, their suffrage campaign grew in strength; by 1914 eleven states permitted them to vote. They received crucial support from prohibitionists, and the Anti-Saloon League, convinced that women voters would support its measures, championed their cause. After spectacular campaigns to dramatize their plight, which included picketing the White House, women obtained their long-sought demand in the Nineteenth Amendment adopted August 26, 1920.

Partisan politics was attacked from still another quarter, from those who felt that greater efficiency in both public administration and private business was the solution to the country's problems. The broadening scientific and technical horizons of the Progressive Era nourished a generation of men who glimpsed what could be done if both private and public decisions were made more efficiently. They looked upon the current political system—conflicts among pressure groups as well as partisan strife—as slipshod; they equally distrusted greater popular participation in making decisions about complicated and technical questions. Efficient action required freedom from these pressures of self-interest which might lead to decisions different from those required by scientific and technical knowledge. A government of expanded functions in which the power of decision lay in the hands of experts could transcend the "petty" bickerings of political strife, rise above a welter of grassroots interests, and produce the greatest good for society as a whole. The politics of the gospel of efficiency implied a drastic shift in the method of making public decisions and an equally drastic shift in the location of political power.

This political process achieved its highest expression in the conservation movement. Inspired by Theodore Roosevelt and led by a group of federal scientists and technicians in his administration, conservation involved an ambitious federal program for the most efficient development and use of the country's natural resources. Although these leaders dealt mainly with the development of western public lands and navigable streams, they worked closely with the engineering societies, the scientific-management movement, and those in private business who championed efficiency and fought waste. Through the United States Forest Service under the dynamic and inspiring Chief Forester Gifford Pinchot (1865–1946) and the Department of the Interior under James R. Garfield (1865–1950), federal officials experimented with scientific planning in which each piece of public land would be developed to its highest potential use. The ideas of the Newlands Reclamation Act of 1902, which provided federal aid for western irrigation development, were expanded into a program of multiple-purpose development—flood control, navigation, water power, and irrigation—of all the nation's rivers under a single authority. The basic political element of these programs lay in the implication that decisions about resource management should be made by technicians guided by standards of efficiency rather than by contests for political power among many competing interests arising from the grass roots.

Yet conservation leaders did not realize this hope. Each attempt to establish a technical decision-making body withered under the incessant demand by grass-roots organizations to exercise control over the resource program they desired. A federal range-management proposal failed because of the opposition of western settlers who argued that land which range scientists thought best fit for grazing actually could be farmed. A multiple-purpose water program collapsed as each interest group, seeking influence and power in resource management, obtained from Congress a special program for its particular concern, be it flood control, drainage, reclamation, or navigation. The federal agencies that carried out these single-purpose programs became directly responsive to the clientele they served and hardly conformed to the ideal of the technicians. Those federal conservation agencies which possessed some original semblance of independence soon came to be battlegrounds for conflicts among many interest groups.

THE SUPREME COURT

The United States Supreme Court plays a role equal to that of the legislature and the executive in making public decisions. In the process of judicial review the Court goes far beyond merely interpreting the meaning of legislation to declare whether or not laws are constitutional. This power is essentially political; the Court can thwart reforms which even the legislature has approved. Supreme Court Justices, moreover, face no effective check upon their decisions; their power is limited solely by a difficult and rarely used process of constitutional amendment and by their own sense of judicial self-restraint. During the Progressive Era the Court declared unconstitutional many laws that reformers desired. In turn, those whose demands the Court rejected vigorously attacked the entire procedure of judicial review and launched a campaign for measures to check the power of the Justices.

In the decades following the Civil War the Supreme Court fashioned a body of new constitutional doctrine with which it struck down numerous laws regulating private business. The constitutional basis for this new doctrine lay in the first section of the Fourteenth Amendment, adopted in 1868: "nor shall any State deprive any person of life, liberty, or property without due process of law. . . ." Although Congress originally designed the "due process" clause to protect the legal rights of the recently freed slaves, the Supreme Court, responding to the postwar public apathy toward civil rights for Negroes, interpreted it so narrowly as to render it ineffective for that purpose. On the other hand, reflecting the prevailing climate of opinion favorable to business growth, the Court read into the due process clause an entirely new meaning which served to protect private business from public regulation.

This transition came in several stages. In *Munn* v. *Illinois* (1877) Justice Stephen J. Field first enunciated the view that the due process clause protected private business from state regulation, except that states, in accordance with past court decisions though not specifically provided for in the Constitution, had certain "police powers" to protect the health, morals, and welfare of its citizens and toward that end could restrict business. Although this was a minority opinion, the Court's majority gradually accepted Field's argument. In the Santa Clara case in 1886, moreover, the Court made clear its view that within the meaning of the due process clause of the Fourteenth Amendment a corporation became a legal person and therefore was subject to its protection. To widen the scope of the clause, the Court argued that "liberty" referred not, as previously, merely to liberty of person but also to freedom to use one's faculties, to dispose of one's property, and to contract with others as one saw fit. In *Lochner* v. *New York* (1905) the Court struck down a law limiting to ten the daily working hours for bakers on the ground that it infringed freedom of contract within the meaning of the due process clause. The opinion in the Lochner case is a classic expression of the new viewpoint; by this time the Court had fully read into the Constitution a new meaning designed to protect business from regulation.

Through its interpretation of the interstate commerce clause of the Constitution the Court struck down federal regulation as well. In 1890 Congress passed the Sherman Antitrust Act under its general power to regulate commerce "among the several states." In the E. C. Knight case (1895), involving monopoly in sugar refining, the Court ruled that the Sherman Act did not apply to production; production was clearly not commerce and therefore was subject solely to state regulation. Later cases involving laws that regulated business by regulating goods flowing in interstate commerce met a similar fate; in 1918 the Court struck down the Keating-Owen Child Labor Law of 1916, which prohibited shipment in interstate commerce of goods manufactured by child labor, on the grounds that it attempted to regulate production and therefore to exercise power reserved to the states. The Court accepted some laws regulating the flow of products in interstate commerce—women in the white-slave traffic, for example, and lottery tickets—on the grounds that these were "bad" products. However, it made no attempt to define good or bad products and retained for itself the power so to distinguish in each individual case.

By nullifying both state and federal regulatory laws, the Supreme Court created a no man's land in which private business faced a minimum of restriction. In response, from those groups which sought legislation to lessen the impact of industrialism a great outcry arose to check the Court's power. The Justices, they argued, had transformed the Court into a third House of Congress, ruling on the reasonableness of laws rather than upon the legislature's power to enact them. Such policy matters were legislative rather than judicial and should be left to elected representatives to decide.

The Politics of Adjustment

Those who objected to the Court's rulings demanded constitutional amendments to change its decisions; the Sixteenth Amendment, for example, which provided a constitutional basis for the income tax, prevented the Court from again nullifying an income-tax law as it had done in 1895. A demand arose for the popular recall of judges and judicial decisions as a check upon the Court's power; in the campaign of 1912 Theodore Roosevelt took up this proposal. Only in this way, it was argued, could the popular will overcome the Court's attempt to thwart democracy.

Against this torrent of criticism others revolted. Already disturbed by the movement to limit representative government through more direct democracy, men such as President Taft argued that judicial recall would destroy the last vestige of representative institutions and would expose property and individuals to the whims of popular outcry. Since Taft was already disgusted with popular outbursts against his own administration, which he felt to be unreasoned and unjust, he was in no mood to trust the "popular will." To such men as Taft the Supreme Court, by interpreting the fundamental law of the land, provided the stability needed in a political system otherwise subject to shifting and impulsive moods. To attack the Court was to attack the very foundation of American institutions.

This view closely reflected the traditional American political ideology that the Constitution was akin to divine law and the judges high priests who interpreted it. But the Court's hostility to reform legislation persuaded an increasing number of Americans to question its sanctity. Did not judges interpret the fundamental law of the land through their own eyes and their own preconceptions? Charles Beard (1874–1948), in his *An Economic Interpretation of the Constitution* (1913), maintained that the Constitution-makers, far from responding to divine inspiration, intentionally fashioned a

The Response to Industrialism

basic law that would protect the dominant economic interests of the day against popular tendencies to restrain wealth. In a far less sensational manner, Oliver Wendell Holmes, Jr. (1841–1935), Justice of the Supreme Court, argued that the common law had developed in response to the "felt necessities of the time" rather than as a reflection of divine law and that the Supreme Court could not afford to resist newer points of view.

The furor over the Court's attitude obscured the extent to which it approved a number of important reforms of the Progressive Era. The Court accepted legislation to regulate railroad rates and services and approved almost all the new natural-resource policies as a legitimate exercise of federal authority over federal property. Although it did not proceed in labor legislation as rapidly as many desired, and was prone to confine labor-union activity to narrow bounds, the Court became convinced that long hours of work endangered the health and welfare of workers and approved laws to regulate them. While restraining many impulses of the time, therefore, the Justices retained sufficient flexibility to look with favor upon a number of innovations.

VIII. The Rise to World Power

As the United States grew in industrial might, it rose to greater prominence on the world scene and assumed a more positive and vigorous role in international affairs. During the nineteenth century Americans had turned their energies toward internal economic development. In the eighties and nineties they increasingly engaged in economic, strategic, and cultural enterprises abroad and demanded that their government protect and promote their new ventures. Diplomacy revealed that the nation entered upon this task without a sustained foreign policy. At times it plunged headlong into the intricacies of international politics; just as frequently it drew back, hesitating to undertake the obligations accompanying closer ties with other countries. Yet through this vacillation ran a continuous thread: American penetration into many areas around the globe drove the United States irresistibly toward more active participation in world affairs.

THE ELEMENTS OF EXPANSION

Economic expansion played a crucial role in this rise to world power. Foreign commerce, not large in proportion to total production, increased rapidly toward the end of the century. While exports just after the Civil War hardly reached $400,000,000 annually, by World War I they came to $2,500,000,000 a year. Exports of agricultural products and raw materials declined, while those of industrial goods, especially steel, oil, tobacco, and textiles, sharply increased. Imports rose as rapidly as did exports; in response to the increasing needs of an industrial economy, foodstuffs and industrial raw materials soon replaced manufactured goods as the major items purchased from abroad.

In the late 1890's when American businessmen became enthusiastic about the possibilities of increasing their foreign sales, their attention fell on the untapped markets of eastern Asia, South America, and Canada. Measures which the business community proposed testify to these aspirations: consular service reform to stress ability rather than political appointments and to emphasize more effective promotion of American products abroad; an isthmian canal to shorten the distance to Far Eastern and western South American markets; a Pacific cable to facilitate communications with Pacific consumers; a federal bureau to promote foreign trade by collecting statistical information concerning market opportunities—finally obtained in the Department of Commerce and Labor (1903); and tariff reciprocity, that the United States open foreign markets by agreeing to lower its tariff if other countries would do the same. Businessmen were not without influence on American foreign policy, and in foreign countries they often worked closely with consular agents who, in effect, represented American enterprise.

Foreign investments, though of less importance than commercial contacts, increased as well. In 1900 American investments abroad amounted to only $455,000,000; by 1914 the figure reached some $2,500,000,000. Capitalists increasingly sought concessions from foreign governments to build railroads, develop mines, and establish fruit plantations. Their pleas for American protection for their concessions met with only slight success; yet they added considerably to the influences which directed the State Department's attention to those areas where American stakes were highest. After 1909, moreover, the State Department promoted foreign investment to further strategic objectives.

These new economic contacts helped to broaden the American sphere of interest and to generate a larger concept of national security. Special emphasis was placed on a new navy and far-flung naval bases. The navy, though permitted to deteriorate rapidly after the Civil War, was rebuilt beginning in the early 1880's. Successive Secretaries of the Navy, notably Benjamin Tracy during the Harrison administration, demanded that modern steel warships be substituted for old wooden vessels. Congress authorized four steel ships in 1883; succeeding administrations continued the program until by 1909 the United States had moved from twelfth to second rank among the world's navies. This program faced many obstacles—the lack of manufacturing facilities for rolling steel ship plates, prejudices within the navy against armored cruising vessels and in favor of sail, concepts of naval warfare which emphasized commerce raiding and passive coast defense as the main wartime function of a navy, and midwestern opposition to appropriations which helped seacoast shipbuilding centers rather than interior areas.

Admiral Alfred T. Mahan (1840–1914) of the Naval War College rose to combat this opposition. In the *Influence of Sea Power on History* (1890), Mahan not only argued that national prosperity and destiny depended on commercial expansion and accompanying naval protection but also proposed a new theory of naval strategy emphasizing a strong offensive navy to prevent a blockade during war. Although Mahan was a prolific writer, he wielded more influence in naval and government circles than with the general public; Americans absorbed much of his writings about "destiny" but little of his more specific naval theory. Theodore Roosevelt contributed even more to the cause of the new American navy. Aided by the Navy League, organized in 1902, Roosevelt not only increased the navy's size but improved its quality. He insisted on greater efficiency in construction and operation; he promoted a program to increase the number of officers and seamen and to improve their training; he reorganized the fleet into two major fighting forces, the Atlantic Fleet and the Pacific Fleet.

Those who transmitted American institutions and customs to foreign lands proved to be no less important in setting the tone of expansion. Americans deeply believed in the innate superiority of Anglo-Saxon peoples and of their political, economic, and religious institutions. To the enthusiastic audiences who heard him speak and read his books on American history, John Fiske imparted his conviction that the political genius of Aryan peoples was the hope of the world. The eloquent imperialist, Senator Albert J. Beveridge (1862–1927) from Indiana, spoke in more flamboyant language: "God has not been preparing the English-speaking and Teutonic peoples for a thousand years for nothing but vain and idle self-contemplation. . . . He has made us the master organizers of the world to establish system where chaos reigns. . . . He has made us adepts in government that we may administer government among savages and senile peoples."

Many agreed with the Congregational clergyman Josiah Strong, who combined this Anglo-Saxon myth with an expanded version of the Darwinian struggle for existence to prophesy an impending racial conflict in which the innately superior Anglo-Saxons would emerge supreme. Fear of the "Yellow Peril" from Asia accompanied the pleas of Roosevelt and Mahan for a larger navy and for territorial acquisitions. America, moreover, so the argument ran, should transmit this superior civilization to less fortunate people, should take up the "white man's burden" and civilize the savages. This was the keynote of "manifest destiny," a missionary enterprise involving an air of superiority and condescension which drove a deep wedge between the United States and peoples of the Orient and Latin America. "Manifest destiny" was especially popular in the 1890's; yet it persisted in a less flamboyant manner for many years.

This air of superiority reached foreigners through diplomats, businessmen, missionaries, and a sprinkling of travelers, as well as through the events of international politics. Few United States official representatives abroad bothered to learn the native language, and fewer still tried to earn the personal friendship of "foreigners." The gap in standards of living frequently separated Americans from other peoples, and racial prejudice toward Indians and Negroes in Latin America and Orientals in the Far East served further to segregate the two communities. Americans held different attitudes toward Latin-Americans and Far Easterners on the one hand and Europeans on the other. The State Department frequently reserved legations in South America for deserving politicians and adopted a tone of communication far more abrupt and demanding toward South American nations than toward western European countries. Businessmen sent abroad both inferior products and agents whom they could not place in the States. Although Protestant missionaries were far more anxious to establish close contact with others, they could scarcely conceal their repugnance toward what they considered to be the inferior non-Christian religions of the Pacific and the Orient and the Catholic faith in Latin America. To Protestant missionaries in Asia, for example, non-Christian Chinese were simply heathen who had to be saved from damnation. Seldom did citizens of the United States accept and appreciate people of other countries in their own right.

The nation did not plunge overnight into international politics; yet the new Large Policy abroad became unmistakably clear. In its conduct of foreign relations the State Department defined more broadly the geographical scope of the national interest and relied more frequently upon armed force to realize the country's new ambitions. But many were reluctant to support these new interests extensively with power outside the Western Hemisphere, and they feared overt alliances with other nations. American international politics often seemed to involve bumptious bluster, "waving the big stick," rather than persistent and determined support of a reasoned national interest. The United States approached world power spasmodically and with a guilty conscience. Yet every President of the time, from the jingoist Theodore Roosevelt to the principled anti-imperialist Grover Cleveland, found it impossible to resist American expansion.

THE CARIBBEAN

The Caribbean area, which the United States had long considered to be its sphere of interest, was most affected by American expansion. In the Monroe Doctrine, enunciated first in 1823, President Monroe had announced that his country did not consider the Western Hemisphere subject to colonization by other nations. Many times thereafter the United States protested when European nations displayed a political interest in Central and Latin America. Until the twentieth century, however, application of the Monroe Doctrine remained essentially negative and limited to preventive action. The new spirit of expansion transformed this negative approach into a positive program in which the United States supported claims to a sphere of influence with actual power and crystallized its Caribbean policy around the protection of the Panama Canal.

This new departure first appeared in the foreign policy of James G. Blaine, Secretary of State under President Garfield and again under President Harrison. Blaine championed more vigorous action to expand American economic and political influence in Latin America. He sought reciprocal trade agreements to promote markets for American industry, arbitration treaties to provide the political stability essential for foreign trade, and Pan-American conferences— the first held in 1889—to foster closer ties between the two areas. Blaine sought naval bases throughout the Caribbean, revived interest in purchasing the Danish West Indies, and promoted construction of a canal across Central America.

United States interest in a more positive policy in the Caribbean quickened with the Venezuelan crisis of 1895. The dispute involved a long-standing disagreement between Great Britain and Venezuela over the boundary between British Guiana and Venezuela and aroused the American public to denounce England bitterly. President Cleveland, responding to this pressure, dispatched a sharp note to England demanding arbitration of the controversy. When the British Foreign Office replied in an equally caustic manner, even denying the validity of the Monroe Doctrine, Cleveland recommended to Congress that the United States itself take steps to establish the correct boundary and to enforce it. The two countries appeared perilously close to war over a seemingly trivial incident. But England, diplomatically isolated in Europe and in need of friendship in the Western Hemisphere, soon agreed to arbitrate, and the incident was amicably settled.

The Cuban revolt against Spain riveted the attention of the United States even more firmly on the Caribbean. In striking contrast to their lack of interest in the Cuban insurrection of 1868–78,

The Response to Industrialism

Americans expressed warm approval of the revolutionaries of 1895–98. Brutal methods which the Spanish used to suppress the revolt—differing little from their opponents' techniques, but more widely publicized—aroused much sympathy for the Cubans. The American "yellow press," especially William Randolph Hearst's *Journal* and Joseph Pulitzer's *World*, bitter rivals in New York City, eagerly played up Cuban atrocity stories. The American people avidly consumed this sensationalism; during 1898 the *Journal*'s daily circulation rose from 800,000 to 1,500,000. The popular demand for intervention in Cuba increased in February, 1898, when the battleship "Maine" exploded in Havana Harbor with a loss of over 250 men. Although its cause was never established, Americans immediately blamed Spain for this tragedy. The administration, though peaceful in intent and bearing, could not withstand such public sentiment. The American people rapidly brushed aside Spanish overtures to settle the matter on terms close to American demands, and Congress eagerly approved McKinley's request for war. In a brief encounter, remembered by most Americans as the war in which Theodore Roosevelt led his Rough Riders in a well-publicized charge up San Juan Hill, the American forces rapidly overwhelmed the weaker Spaniards; at the Paris Peace Conference in 1898 Cuba became independent, and the United States acquired the Philippines, Guam, and Puerto Rico.

Caribbean diplomacy after the Spanish-American War centered around the construction and defense of an isthmian canal. Dramatic illustration of the need for such a project came during the Spanish-American War when the battleship "Oregon" steamed from Puget Sound around Cape Horn—three times the distance had a canal been available—to join the main squadron off Cuba. In Central American diplomacy prior to the 1880's, the United States had concentrated on preventing other nations from building a canal without American co-operation. In 1850, for example, the Clayton-Bulwer Treaty with England had provided that neither nation would carry out the project alone. As the American eagle spread its wings wider in the post–Civil War era, interest arose in an "American canal under American control." The commitment to joint construction, however, blocked the movement. Efforts to annul the Clayton-Bulwer Treaty, initiated as early as 1881, did not succeed until 1901; in the second Hay-Pauncefote Treaty of that year, England freed the United States from its obligation.

The canal project also had to clear a maze of Latin-American diplomacy and intrigue. In the Spooner Act of 1902 Congress approved the Panama instead of the Nicaragua route, and the following year Hay signed the Hay-Herran Convention in which Colombia, owner of Panama, granted the United States the right to construct the canal. The Colombian Congress rejected the Hay-Herran pact, despite a virtual United States ultimatum that Colombia would "regret" it if she did not ratify the convention without modification. Colombians objected that it provided only slender compensation and seriously compromised their nation's sovereignty. Thereupon the Panamanians revolted from Colombia on November 3, 1903. The U.S.S. "Nashville" conveniently appeared on the scene to prevent Colombia from suppressing the revolt, and Secretary John Hay (1838–1905) warned that the United States would not tolerate Colombian steps to restore authority over the area. The administration knew of the impending event, hoped that it would succeed, and, as Hay put it, was "not to be caught napping." Roosevelt later boasted, "I took the Canal Zone," an exaggeration but close to the truth. One hour after receiving news of the revolt, Roosevelt authorized that the new government be recognized, and on November 18 the two countries signed the Hay-Bunau-Varilla Treaty granting the United States the desired canal rights. By 1914 the Panama Canal was open for traffic. In 1916 the United States completed its canal diplomacy when in the Bryan-Chamorro Treaty it secured from Nicaragua a perpetual right to construct a waterway through that country.

The entire Caribbean area now became crucial to the national defense of the United States. As one commentator observed, "No matter how strongly the isthmian canal may be fortified it would, in war, serve us no purpose . . . if our fleet could not control its approaches." The United States quickly established naval bases in the Caribbean and secured greater political control over its bordering countries to guarantee influence in the area "at least to the extent deemed necessary to prevent its domination by any other strong power." In effect the Caribbean became a dependency of a United States which would not tolerate basic decisions contrary to its interests and would use force to guarantee that end. During the first three decades of the twentieth century the United States repeatedly intervened in Caribbean countries and established a number of protectorates there.

After the Spanish-American War, Cuba was in form independent; in fact, she became a satellite in the United States orbit. The Platt Amendment to the army appropriation bill of March 2, 1901, guaranteed this. Passed when it appeared that the Cuban constitutional convention would ignore Cuban–United States relations, the Platt Amendment provided that Cuba could not permit a foreign power to secure even partial control there, that she could not incur an indebtedness that might result in foreign intervention, that the United States could step in to preserve order and maintain Cuban independence, and that Cuba would sell or lease naval and coaling stations to the United States. The Cubans reluctantly incorporated the Platt Amendment into their constitution in June, 1901, after they had been told, in effect, that the United States would not otherwise withdraw its army from Cuba. To prevent Cuba from eliminating the agreement by constitutional amendment after departure of the military government, the United States in 1903 successfully insisted that it be incorporated into a treaty between the two nations.

Other protectorates followed in rapid order. In the Hay-Bunau-Varilla Treaty, for example, the United States permanently guaranteed the territorial integrity and independence of Panama. Protectorates stemmed most frequently from a fear that European nations might attempt forcibly to collect debts owed them by Caribbean governments. Creditors had rarely been pleased with the repayment records of shaky Latin-American regimes. In exasperation, England, Germany, and Italy in 1902 forcibly sought to persuade the Venezuelan dictator Cipriano Castro to come to terms. In settling this incident the World Court two years later ruled that those creditors who had used force had claims prior to those who had not. This decision greatly alarmed the State Department, for it seemed to place a premium on armed intervention to collect Western Hemisphere debts. In 1904 a similar situation seemed on the point of erupting in Santo Domingo. This time the Roosevelt administration worked out an agreement with the Dominican government in which the United States assumed control of the customs service and apportioned 55 per cent of its receipts to repay European creditors.

On this occasion the President enunciated the "Roosevelt Corollary" to the Monroe Doctrine: henceforth when the internal affairs of nations of the Western Hemisphere might be such as to encourage European intervention, the United States itself would intervene to forestall such action. As Roosevelt announced in his message to Congress on December 6, 1904, "Chronic wrongdoing . . . may force the United States, however reluctantly . . . to the exercise of

an international police power." The implications of the Roosevelt
Corollary soon became clear. The original financial protectorate in
the Dominican Republic had been established in co-operation with
Dominican political leaders. By 1916, however, no candidate for the
Dominican presidency could be found who would agree to the abso-
lute authority of the United States on the island. From 1916 to
1922, accordingly, the United States Department of the Navy governed that republic.

The State Department soon came to look upon United States
business interests in the Caribbean as allies in political control; they
could drive out European businessmen, establish closer economic
ties between Caribbean countries and the United States, and aid in
promoting political stability in an area torn with frequent strife.
American businessmen were not averse to such a policy; they often
wanted to go even further and secure outright annexation of areas in
which their investments were at stake. Throughout the nineteenth
century economic and strategic expansion had been closely intertwined; in the twentieth century the United States took up a more
self-conscious encouragement and protection of economic ties with
Caribbean countries to undergird political strategy.

Roosevelt carried out this policy, soon known popularly as "Dollar Diplomacy," in Cuba, Ecuador, and Bolivia; President Taft and
his Secretary of State, Philander C. Knox, used it more extensively
to establish protectorates in Central America. In 1909, for example,
Secretary Knox prevented the Nicaraguan government from quell-
ing a revolt and then demanded control of the customs from the new
government and persuaded it to transfer the public debt from European to United States creditors. President Wilson continued Caribbean "Dollar Diplomacy"; in 1915 American troops occupied
Haiti, and the Senate approved a treaty which granted control of the
Haitian customs to the United States, established an American

financial adviser, and secured from Haiti an agreement never to lease or sell territory to a third power.

The United States also assumed more vigorous leadership in settling disputes between Latin-American countries. Two objectives lay behind this: to promote the political stability essential for both economic penetration and military strategy and to prevent European nations from becoming peacemakers in Latin America in order to gain influence there. In 1906, at President Roosevelt's instigation, the chief executives of Mexico and the United States intervened to promote settlement of a war between Guatemala and Honduras. The following year, when another Central American war appeared imminent, the same two leaders called a Central American Peace Conference which established a Central American Court of Justice to settle international disputes. The experiment was successful; no international war in Central America took place after 1907. Although the court failed to end two revolutions, its prestige remained high until the United States itself became a party to its demise. When Nicaragua signed the Bryan-Chamorro Treaty with the United States in 1914, Costa Rica, Honduras, and El Salvador maintained that their rights had been ignored; they brought to the court a case against Nicaragua. Although the judges decided in favor of the claimants, both Nicaragua and the United States refused to accept the verdict.

Latin-Americans did not respond with favor to the new behavior of the Colossus of the North. Despite the fact that the United States often undertook protectorates reluctantly and refused to undertake others, the implications of its new Caribbean interests were clear. Latin-Americans had never accepted the Monroe Doctrine; frequently they had sought greater French and English influence in the Western Hemisphere to check the ambitions of the United States. But the British-American rapprochement, leaving the United States a free hand in the Caribbean, appeared to Latin-Americans to abandon them to face their northern neighbor alone. Their fate became even clearer when Germany and other nations expressly told Colombia that they would not interfere with Roosevelt's Panamanian coup and when in the Roosevelt Corollary the President announced his intention to intervene in internal affairs in the Caribbean if necessary.

Latin-Americans viewed the Platt Amendment as an infringement on Cuban liberty which the United States might in the future extend to other nations. When President Wilson refused to recognize a *de facto* revolutionary government in Mexico simply because he felt that it was not truly representative, they had further cause to fear intervention from the north. But the Panama incident had aroused most resentment. Latin-American nations only belatedly recognized the new republic. In 1912 the United States minister to Colombia explained that, as a result of the Panama incident, "the friendship of nearly a century disappeared, the indignation of every Colombian, and millions of other Latin-Americans, was aroused and is still most intensely active." To counteract growing hostility Secretary of State Root in 1906 undertook a "good-will" tour of Latin America, and in 1912 Secretary Knox repeated the performance. Though manifestations of friendship accompanied these visits, resentment smoldered inwardly. Latin-Americans continued to speak of "blah-blah" Pan-Americanism, and not until the "Good Neighbor Policy" of the 1930's did relations between the rival areas improve.

THE PACIFIC

The United States had long considered the Samoan and Hawaiian Islands to be within its sphere of interest. Prior to the Civil War American naval officers, merchants, and missionaries had established footholds there. Although anxious to prevent other nations from acquiring the islands, the United States was unwilling to do so itself. Toward the end of the century, however, this negative policy gave way to positive support for American interests in both island groups and to eventual annexation.

The United States especially prized the harbor of Pago Pago in the Samoan Islands, an archipelago which commands important ocean lanes in the South Pacific. In 1878 Samoa granted the Americans rights to a naval station at Pago Pago. Although the United States did not seek to annex the islands, in 1887 she prevented England and Germany from acquiring them. In the Berlin Act two years later the three powers established a tripartite protectorate, nominally guaranteeing Samoa "autonomy and independence" but reserving the right of each to interfere in every legislative act that might affect foreigners. Continued rivalry among the three powers in Samoa led to a new accord in 1899 in which Germany and the United States divided the islands between them, and England received concessions elsewhere. The Samoan acquisition stemmed in part from the "manifest destiny" enthusiasm of the 1890's. Yet it was also the logical culmination of years of interest in the islands, an unwillingness to forgo American influence there, and the pressure of international rivalries which forced the United States to act to protect its sphere of interest.

Business and missionary activities in Hawaii also dated from before the Civil War; they expanded rapidly after a commercial reciprocity treaty of 1875 opened American markets to Hawaiian sugar. The navy, moreover, increasingly prized Pearl Harbor as a naval base, exclusive rights to which the United States acquired when the two nations renewed the commercial treaty in 1887. These substantial interests gave rise to the view that Hawaii came within the sphere of influence of the United States, that "Hawaii must be an American possession, if it were to become anyone's possession." Toward the end of the nineteenth century evidence increased that if the United States remained aloof, imperial rivalry would prompt other nations to move in.

Tension within Hawaii between native and foreigner in the early 1890's invited such intervention and forced the United States to act. Foreign residents in Hawaii, fearful of a native political regime potentially hostile to their influence, in 1887 forced a new constitution upon the Hawaiian king. In 1893 the new queen, Liliuokalani, more determined than her predecessor to preserve native Hawaiian institutions, tried to annul this document and to restore full native rule. The foreigners immediately revolted and sought protection for their new government by annexation to the United States. The Harrison administration signed a treaty of annexation with Hawaii in short order. However, President Cleveland, who took office shortly thereafter, believed that the American minister and marines had used improper influence to prevent Liliuokalani from suppressing the uprising; he withdrew the treaty. His more receptive successor, William McKinley, signed a second pact which the Senate accepted in 1898.

Acquisition of the Philippines stemmed not from long-standing substantial interests but from timely action by one man, Theodore Roosevelt. As Assistant Secretary of the Navy during the McKinley administration Roosevelt had dispatched Admiral George Dewey (1837–1917) to the Pacific to pounce upon Manila once the United States had opened war against Spain in Cuba. Until Dewey easily defeated the Spanish fleet in Manila Harbor, the people of the United States had known little about the Philippines; in entering the war they had thought of a Cuban crusade rather than a venture into Asian affairs. Roosevelt's action, however, forced the Philippines and the entire Far East into the diplomacy and strategy of the

The Rise to World Power

United States. After the war, President McKinley at first hesitated to retain the islands; when it became clear that self-denial would only render them ripe for picking by another power and that Manila might play an important role in Far Eastern trade and politics, the administration abandoned independence for the Philippines in favor of annexation. The Senate, moreover, in approving this action, defeated a proposal to grant independence in the immediate future.

This turn of events marked a new departure in foreign affairs. The increased tempo of activity in the Caribbean and the South Pacific constituted a new positive policy in a region long considered to be "within the area of the physical and political geography of the United States." Acquisition of the Philippines, on the other hand, greatly widened the nation's sphere of interest to include all of East Asia, and drew it into the realm of Far Eastern power politics long before it was prepared to undertake such new ventures. The public hesitated to use military force to protect the new foothold in Asia; American economic and missionary interests there, though vocal, were hardly strong enough to influence Far Eastern powers or to resist European expansion in the area. In its Far Eastern policy, therefore, the United States was confined to bluster and protest. Even Roosevelt by 1906 expressed the wish that the country could be rid of this Achilles' heel.

The new interests of the United States in the Far East inevitably drew the nation into the tangled web of imperial rivalries in China. In the late nineteenth century Great Britain, Germany, Russia, France, and Japan competed for concessions, spheres of influence, naval bases, and territory in the weak and tottering Chinese empire. To protect its interests in the Far East, the United States in turn sought to prevent the dismemberment of China and to counteract the demand for exclusive concessions by a plea for an "open door" for commercial enterprise in the empire. Such views dovetailed nicely with those of American missionaries and businessmen in eastern Asia. Textile manufacturers who dominated the North China textile trade, capitalists who sought railroad concessions in China, and steel manufacturers who hoped to capture the new market for steel when the railroads were constructed all became worried lest economic opportunities in the Orient be lost.

With such problems in mind, Secretary of State Hay in 1899 dispatched to six major world powers the first of two Open Door notes, a plea for equal commercial opportunity in China. In their replies the six powers indicated many reservations to such a viewpoint, but the Secretary blithely announced that they had agreed to uphold the principle. The following year, during the antiforeign Boxer revolt in Peking, Hay bestirred himself again. Much to the relief of American businessmen and missionaries in the Far East, he sent 2,500 marines to join the armed forces of other powers to relieve the foreign embassies from their Boxer besiegers. But Hay also feared that intervention might lead to infringement of Chinese sovereignty; to forestall such an event he dispatched a second Open Door note, declaring that the United States intended to support not only commercial opportunity but the territorial integrity of China as well. President McKinley revealed the tentativeness of American activity in the Far East when, much to the dismay of Americans in China, he ordered the marines home; the President had a fall election on his hands.

At the turn of the century Russian expansion into Manchuria constituted the major disturbing influence in the Orient. Running athwart Japanese ambitions in the same area, Russian advances touched off the Russo-Japanese War of 1904–5. Winning this conflict, the Japanese displaced Russia as the rising power of East Asia. Foreign policies of the United States shifted in accordance with the changing Asiatic scene. Prior to the Russo-Japanese War Americans had feared Russia more, and upon the outbreak of that conflict our sympathies had been with Japan. When Japan won the war, however, such leaders as President Roosevelt began to look upon that nation as the major threat to our interests in the Far East. When Japan invited Roosevelt to mediate in the war, the President accepted, hoping to prevent the victors from gaining too much at the peace settlement. At the Portsmouth, New Hampshire, peace conference Japan abandoned both a large indemnity claim and a demand for the northern half of the island of Sakhalin.

Unable to use military strength to withstand Japanese expansion after 1905, Roosevelt resorted to diplomacy to divert that nation from the Philippines, even if it meant partially closing the Open Door. He agreed to acknowledge the legitimacy of Japanese penetration elsewhere if Japan in turn would take no aggressive steps toward the Philippines. In 1905, in the Taft-Katsura executive agreement, Roosevelt recognized Japan's "suzerainty over" Korea —we withdrew our legation and henceforth dealt with the Hermit Kingdom through Japan—and Japan in turn disavowed any hostile ambitions in the Philippines. Three years later, in the Root-Takahira executive accord, the two powers agreed to maintain the status quo in the Pacific, to respect each other's territorial possessions there, to uphold the Open Door in China, and to support the independence and integrity of the Chinese empire.

Japanese-American relations, however, remained discordant. The Japanese blamed the United States for failure to gain more at Portsmouth; they became even more aroused over treatment of their fellow countrymen in the Pacific Coast states. Californians took up an energetic anti-Japanese campaign after the Russo-Japanese War. In October, 1906, the San Francisco Board of Education ordered Orientals to attend segregated public schools. To allay anti-American feeling which this incident aroused in Japan, President Roosevelt persuaded the San Francisco authorities to permit Japanese children to attend school with whites in return for an end to Japanese immigration. In the Gentlemen's Agreement of 1907-8 (a series of diplomatic notes, not a treaty), Japan agreed not to permit immigration of coolies directly to the United States mainland. But this settlement only temporarily quieted feelings on both sides. Californians continued to inflame Japanese-American relations; in 1913 the state legislature effectively barred Japanese from owning land in that state, an action which greatly embarrassed the Wilson administration.

While Roosevelt had tried to placate Japan by giving her free rein on the mainland of Asia, Taft undertook to impede her expansion by applying an Asiatic version of Caribbean Dollar Diplomacy. American capitalists, with little success, had long sought concessions in China and with even less success had requested that the United States government protect their investments. The Taft administration responded to their overtures; under the leadership of Secretary of State Knox, economic expansion and political strategy were joined to augment American influence in the Far East against Japan. Under pressure from the State Department the major European powers in the Far East admitted American bankers to a consortium, or banking group, which financed the Hukuang railways in China. Knox, in turn, promoted a plan to reorganize the Chinese railways in Manchuria. These ventures bore little fruit; but they failed because of wrangling among the parties involved rather than because of lack of interest on the part of American bankers and statesmen.

Differing with both Roosevelt and Taft, President Wilson considered Far Eastern policy not in terms of power politics but from the ideal of self-government for all nations. He denounced Dollar Diplomacy because he feared that it might limit Chinese sovereignty. He chose, instead, to further the creation of an independent China, with a stable government, able to maintain order at home and to withstand pressures from abroad. In 1913 Wilson took the lead in recognizing the new revolutionary government of China which he hoped would be the self-governing republic he sought. Wilson did not cease to encourage investment and commerce in China, for these could contribute stability to the new regime, but he insisted that the State Department not play economic favorites and that instead it promote a general climate conducive to business enterprise. When World War I forced the realities of Far Eastern power politics more sharply upon Wilson, he abandoned this hands-off policy and resorted to Taft's version of Dollar Diplomacy to counteract Japanese expansion on the Asian mainland.

THE PUBLIC REACTION TO EXPANSION

Many Americans did not view with satisfaction the new Large Policy in foreign relations. Not that they opposed greater activity in world affairs; they favored it. But what kind of relationship should the United States establish with other nations? A vigorous assertion of national self-interest and participation in power politics, they feared, did not provide the kind of moral leadership befitting the most vigorous democracy in the world. American ideals rather than its national power should be the instruments of foreign policy; international co-operation rather than competition should be its goal. These critics disagreed with the view that internationalism could not transcend the basic fact of national interest. They felt sure that their moral unity, if activated, could impel all men to rise above their differences and to abolish war. Peace depended not upon an uncertain balance of power and heightened nationalism, but upon the freest possible flow of goods, people, and ideas among countries. Nations could settle their disputes most effectively, not by a show of armed strength, but through enforcement of international law by impartial arbitral commissions and judicial bodies.

These views became increasingly popular in the years after the Spanish-American War. The implications of territorial annexation far from home and a prolonged optimism associated with domestic reform generated a popular peace movement which was hostile to the policies of Roosevelt and Mahan. Americans cheered wildly when a President of this viewpoint, Woodrow Wilson, denounced Dollar Diplomacy in October, 1913: "It is a very perilous thing to determine the foreign policy of a nation in the terms of material interest. . . . Human rights, national integrity, and opportunity as against material interests . . . is the issue which we now have to face." The public eagerly devoured Sir Norman Angell's (1874———) condemnation of war, *The Great Illusion* (1910), while Mahan bitterly complained that Americans would not listen to him, and Roosevelt fulminated against "mushy philanthropists," "visionaries," and "mollycoddles," who did not appreciate the fundamental facts of international life.

Anti-imperialists comprised a variety of groups and individuals: former Liberal Republicans like Carl Schurz, such humanitarians as Jane Addams, and pro-Cleveland Democrats, including the former President himself, who favored free trade, the gold standard as a medium of international exchange, and the elimination of barriers among nations. Especially strong in the Northeast, anti-imperialists first organized in opposition to the proposal to acquire the Philippines. Would not control of a subject people, they argued, violate American traditions of self-government? Was it not ironical that American troops should suppress a Filipino insurrection in 1899 soon after fighting a war to "free" the islands from Spain? Many, such as William Jennings Bryan, who had participated in the great humanitarian crusade to free Cuba now felt that they had been tricked into an imperialist venture. The Anti-Imperialist League, organized in the fall of 1898, fought for a proposal to insure independence for the Philippines and, under Bryan's leadership as the Democratic presidential candidate, carried the issue into the election of 1900. Their efforts failed. Agitation against acquisition of the Philippines faded after the Republican victory in 1900, and by 1905 the League had declined to a small New England organization which survived fitfully until the 1920's.

Full of optimism that war could be abolished, Americans participated actively in a more general peace movement in the decade prior to World War I. Peace societies multiplied in numbers and in membership. The most prominent among these, the American Peace Society, concentrated on disarmament and peaceful methods of resolving international disputes; its members included Bryan and Wilson, philanthropists, journalists, lawyers, and ministers. Women's organizations and such prominent figures as Jane Addams became especially active in the peace crusade. Philanthropists endowed world peace foundations, such as the Carnegie Endowment for International Peace (1910), to which Andrew Carnegie granted ten million dollars; the Carnegie Foundation carried out extensive research on international law, the causes of war, and the work of peace societies in the past. Under the leadership of Rev. John Haynes Holmes, the newly organized Federal Council of the Churches of Christ established a department of peace. College student organizations, such as the Christian Students Federation, inspired thousands of young people with the ideal of human brotherhood. And in 1907 the American School Peace League was organized to tone down the emphasis on wars in school textbooks.

These organizations attacked Dollar Diplomacy, the naval construction program, and other elements of American balance-of-power politics; more important, they championed measures of their own to reduce international tension. Representatives of the United States persuaded the Hague Peace Conference in 1899 to establish the Hague Permanent Court of Arbitration; governments, if they desired, could submit disputes to this body. This experiment soon languished for want of cases to review; but in 1902, at the request of peace groups, Theodore Roosevelt gave the court a boost by submitting to it a long-standing conflict over economic claims by California against Mexico. Efforts to increase the court's functions and to promote disarmament at a Second Hague Conference in 1907 did not succeed. Although its activity was not spectacular, the court served as a major focus of the pre–World War I peace movement.

Peace advocates had long urged countries to adopt treaties in which the signatories bound themselves to arbitrate certain types of disputes. Many felt in the 1890's that a permanent arbitration treaty would have prevented the furor between Great Britain and the United States over the Venezuelan boundary. Consequently, in 1897 these two countries signed a general arbitration agreement. But the Senate, demanding that the United States not yield an inch of sovereignty in the interests of world peace, exempted from the treaty most types of controversies and then required that no issue could be submitted for arbitration without a two-thirds affirmative Senate vote. In the final vote the Senate defeated even this amended form of the treaty.

The Hague Court stimulated renewed interest in arbitration treaties. Although Roosevelt and Taft negotiated a great number of these, some exempting from arbitration all disputes affecting the "vital interest, the independence, or the honor of the two contracting states," the Senate three times refused to approve. William Jennings Bryan, Wilson's Secretary of State, achieved greater success with a different type of treaty. Bryan, an ardent Christian pacifist and an admirer of Tolstoi, had long advocated the use of joint commissions to determine disputed facts in international controversies. He now negotiated thirty "cooling-off treaties," providing that every unsolved dispute which might lead to war should be submitted to a permanent commission for investigation. Although the parties were not bound to accept the commission's recommendations, they did agree not to resort to arms until a report appeared. The Senate approved some twenty-two of these pacts, of which many remained in force on the eve of World War II. Bryan considered these treaties to be the most important act of his entire career; in his official portrait at the State Department he holds a copy of one of them.

Neither the "cooling-off treaties" nor the overwhelming interest in peace gave any hint of the impending European crisis which relentlessly drew the United States into World War I. But they did reflect the nation's larger role in international affairs. Those who sought peaceful methods of solving disputes did not wish to draw back into "splendid isolation"; they realized keenly that expansive forces thrust the United States irrevocably upon the world scene, but they sought to prevent these innovations from erupting into nationalistic rivalries and destructive conflict. World War I momentarily and rudely shattered this dream, but the League of Nations and later the United Nations perpetuated its spirit, in the hope that a world more tightly knit by economic and cultural forces could resolve conflicts without war.

IX. The Response to Industrialism

The unifying theme of American history between 1885 and 1914, so many historians have argued, was a popular attack against corporate wealth. Through their state and federal governments, according to this interpretation, the discontented sought to curb corporations and thereby to promote greater economic opportunity for all. This analysis accepts, uncritically, the popular ideas of the Populist-Progressive Era. It is a far too simple explanation.

Industrialism did create disparities in wealth and class divisions beyond our comprehension today. But the social, economic, and political movements of those thirty years reveal something more fundamental and more varied than an attempt by the dispossessed to curb the wealthy. They comprised a reaction not against the corporation alone but also against industrialism and the many ways in which it affected the lives of Americans. The people of that era sought to do much more than simply to control corporations; they attempted to cope with industrial change in all its ramifications. True, they centered their fire on the business leader, but he was a symbol of change which they could conveniently attack, rather than the essence of change itself. A simple interpretation of the discontented poor struggling against the happy rich does violence to the complexity of industrial innovation and to the variety of human striving that occurred in response to it.

In a number of instances, as we have observed in the preceding pages, Americans responded to industrialism in ways far different from those described by many historians. Reforms frequently arose from the well-to-do themselves; the social justice movement, for example, grew up among those who had sufficient leisure to be concerned with education, parks, and the working conditions of women and children. On the other hand, the "people" often opposed the measures which, according to historians, were designed to curb corporate influence. Urban immigrants, for example, resenting the attack on the city political machine, opposed urban civic reforms. In the political upheaval of the 1890's, the industrial workingman refused to join the downtrodden farmer in capturing the Democratic party, and, in one of the greatest political transformations of modern American history, flocked to the Republican party, which was supposedly under corporate domination. It is not surprising that historians, while studying the agrarian revolt in detail, have failed to examine carefully this industrial-urban feature of the political unrest of the early 1890's. To do so would require an admission that rural-urban conflicts were as strong, if not stronger, than the hostility toward corporate wealth.

Although industrial innovation was the common American experience between 1885 and 1914, not all were aware of, or concerned with, the same facets of this change. Manufacturers, merchants, farmers, and workers were most disturbed by the new, impersonal price-and-market economy. The individual enterpriser now felt engulfed by a tidal wave of world-wide influences which he could scarcely understand, let alone control. Those concerned with personal values, on the other hand—religious leaders, women active in public affairs, the new middle class, and the rising group of intellectuals excitedly searching for knowledge about human life—were most impressed with the materialistic bent of industrial society and its hostility to the human spirit. For the millions of people torn from accustomed rural patterns of culture and thrust into a strange, urban environment, the meaning of industrialism lay in a feeling of uprootedness, in the disintegration of old ways of life and the loss of familiar surroundings. Those left behind on the farms experienced the new forces through the expansion of urban culture and its threat to the nation's agrarian traditions. They feared that metropolitan influences would reach out and drastically change the life they knew. Finally, those in the South and West lived under the shadow of a far more highly developed area, which, they felt, deliberately imposed restraints upon the economic growth of their regions.

Industrialism increased the desire for material gain among all Americans; but economic motivation does not wholly explain the behavior of the American people during these years. Industrialism was less important in changing the motives of Americans than in profoundly altering the environment, the setting within which men and women strove for many different goals. Whether one was most concerned with the life of the spirit, with social institutions, or with economic gain, he had to come to terms with the vastly new society brought about by industrialism. The way in which Americans made this adjustment varied according to the positive goals they wished to achieve.

Those with a major concern for economic gain took collective action to influence the price-and-market system and to obtain a larger share of the increased wealth. Those most interested in the life of the free, independent, human spirit feared collective economic action and tried to promote the conditions that would enhance self-reliance, responsibility, and qualities of personal character. Migrants from rural to urban areas sought to create and maintain new ways of group living which would give meaning to their lives in a rapidly moving and impersonal society. Farmers fought back against the cities, often blindly and bitterly, temporarily imposing their patterns of life on the urban areas, but in the long run to no avail. And the South and the West appealed to the federal government for aid in economic growth and for laws to restrict the policies of northeastern corporations and thereby to foster a freer climate in which industry in their section could grow.

Through politics the American people enlisted the aid of public agencies to help solve their problems. Less important in itself, politics was primarily the means whereby people tried to realize their goals in economic, social, intellectual, and religious life. Into the political arena, therefore, were focused all the impulses of these eventful years; and political institutions, as a result, could not remain uninfluenced by industrial change. Political parties and legislative action became the instruments of both industrial growth and the adjustment to industrial innovation. When many found partisan politics ineffective for their purposes, they fashioned new methods of political action.

Industrialism also thrust Americans irrevocably onto the world scene. Some reached out to seek material gain abroad, others to implement an expanded program of national security, and still others as cultural evangelists to spread the American "way of life" to those whom they considered backward. At the same time, the communications revolution drew events abroad closer to the experience of the American people. In the face of such momentous changes, how should Americans respond? Some, arguing that the nation was invincible, demanded that the United States vigorously assert its military might and economic interest. But others believed that foreign policy should strengthen the ties with other peoples rather than divide us from them, and especially that the nation's leaders should explore every possible way of solving disputes peacefully.

Two world wars, the Great Depression of 1929, and a world balancing on the brink of war and self-destruction have blunted our present awareness of the consequences of the events between 1885 and 1914. These later happenings, like industrialism itself, have drastically altered the lives of Americans and forced upon them new types of adjustments. Yet most of the characteristic reactions of the Populist-Progressive Era remain with us today. Occupational groups still seek organization as the answer to their problems, and the struggle among powerful economic groups is an increasingly important fact in the formation of private and public economic policy. Those concerned with personal values and the freedom of individual expression continue to cope with hostile influences, although the threat in more recent years has come as much from the drive for national security as from industrial growth. Cultural and sectional adjustments are often submerged today; yet rural-urban, native-foreign, and sectional differences continue to give rise to major conflicts among the American people. As the twentieth century proceeded, the nation became ever more tightly involved in international life, and the constant threat of being drawn into world war loomed ever more ominously. Yet as early as 1914, many of the later responses to this profound change had already clearly appeared. In foreign as well as in domestic affairs, therefore, the decade of the 1890's was a dividing point in American history, separating the old from the new and setting a pattern for much of the future.

By mid-century it was clear that no nation could escape the revolutionary forces of technology. Other people outside the Western world began to experience the same transformations in their lives which Americans had faced long before. The speed and shock of change were greater, the resistance to innovation often more intense, and the adjustments even more complex and difficult. But beneath these differences lay a common experience that could well serve as a basis for a common understanding among the world's peoples. To the historian there is no more exciting task than to chart the different ways in which industrialism has affected countries all over the world and the varied manner in which different peoples have responded to it. For all of us there is no better method of enlarging our understanding of other nations than to know intimately how we responded to the very forces that millions now face elsewhere.

Important Dates

1862	Federal Department of Agriculture established
	Homestead Act passed
	Morrill Land Grant Act passed
1866–72	National Labor Union
1870–74	Granger movement at its height
1872	Liberal Republican party
1876	Telephone patented by Alexander Graham Bell
1877	*Munn* v. *Illinois;* the Supreme Court approves state laws to regulate railroads
1877–81	Rutherford B. Hayes administration
1878	Greenback party reaches peak strength
1879	Henry George's *Progress and Poverty* published
1881	James A. Garfield administration
1881–85	Chester Alan Arthur administration
1883	Pendleton Civil Service Reform Act passed
1885–86	Knights of Labor organization reaches peak strength
1885–89	Grover Cleveland administration
1886	Haymarket affair in Chicago
	American Federation of Labor organized
1887	Hatch Act passed
	Interstate Commerce Act passed
1888	Edward Bellamy's *Looking Backward* published
1889	First Pan-American Conference held in Washington, D.C.
	Sons of the American Revolution organized
1889–93	Benjamin Harrison administration

Important Dates

1890	Sherman Antitrust Act passed
	General Federation of Women's Clubs organized
	McKinley Tariff Act passed
	Sherman Silver Purchase Act passed
1891	Pope Leo XIII issues encyclical, *Rerum Novarum*
1892	Populist party organized
	Steelworkers strike at Homestead, Pennsylvania
1893–94	American Protective Association reaches peak strength
1893–96	Depression of 1893
1893–97	Cleveland second administration
1894	Coxey's army marches to Washington, D.C.
	National Municipal League organized
	Pullman strike in Chicago
	Immigration Restriction League organized
	Republicans capture Congress for sixteen years
1895	Anti-Saloon League organized.
	United States v. *E. C. Knight Co.*: the Supreme Court refuses to apply the Sherman Antitrust Act to "tight combinations"
	Pollock v. *Farmers' Loan and Trust Co.*; the Supreme Court declares the income tax unconstitutional
	National Association of Manufacturers organized
	Venezuelan boundary dispute
1896	Bryan-McKinley presidential campaign
1897	Maximum Freight Rate case; the Supreme Court demands the right to review the actions of state railroad commissions
1897–1901	William McKinley administration
1897–1904	First industrial consolidation movement in the United States
1898	Spanish-American War
	Anti-Imperialist League organized
	United States annexes Hawaii
	Erdman Act passed
1899	First Open Door note sent by Secretary of State John Hay
	First Hague Conference
	Final partition of Samoa
1900	Boxer revolt against foreigners in China
	Second Open Door note sent by Hay
1901	Platt Amendment passed
	Assassination of President McKinley

The Response to Industrialism

	Second Hay-Pauncefote Treaty
	United States Steel Company organized
1901–9	Theodore Roosevelt administrations
1902	Anthracite coal strike
	Newlands Reclamation Act passed
1903	Hay-Herran Convention
	Panama becomes independent
	Hay-Bunau-Varilla Treaty
	Department of Commerce and Labor established
1903–10	Lincoln Steffens, Ida Tarbell, and others write muckraking articles
1904	American Civic Association organized
	Roosevelt Corollary to Monroe Doctrine
	Northern Securities Company v. *United States;* the first successful prosecution of a "tight combination" under the Sherman Antitrust Act
1905	Portsmouth Peace Conference
	Lochner v. *New York;* the classic statement of the doctrine of substantive due process
	Federal Council of the Churches of Christ organized
1906	Hepburn Act passed
1907	Panic of 1907
	Inland Waterways Commission appointed
	Central American Court of Justice established
	Gentlemen's Agreement with Japan
1908	*Muller* v. *Oregon;* the Supreme Court approves regulation of the hours of work
	Danbury Hatters case; Hatters' Union prosecuted for violating Sherman Antitrust Act
	North American Civic League for Immigrants organized
	White House Conservation Conference
	Country Life Commission established
1909	Payne-Aldrich Tariff Act passed
1909–13	William Howard Taft administration
1910	Mann-Elkins Act passed
	Ballinger-Pinchot controversy
	House curbs Speaker Cannon's powers
1912	Progressive party organized
	Socialist party reaches peak strength

Important Dates

1913   Sixteenth Amendment (Income Tax) ratified
           Seventeenth Amendment (Direct Election of Senators) ratified
           Newlands Arbitration Act passed
           Pujo Committee Report on high finance
           Department of Labor established
           Physical Valuation Act passed
           Webb-Kenyon Interstate Liquor Act passed
           Underwood-Simmons Tariff Act passed
           Federal Reserve Act passed

1913–21   Woodrow Wilson administrations

1914   Bryan-Chamorro Treaty signed, giving United States canal rights through Nicaragua
           Smith-Lever Act provides federal aid for promoting scientific agriculture
           Clayton Antitrust Act passed
           Federal Trade Commission established

1916   Warehouse Act passed
           Keating-Owen Federal Child Labor Act passed
           Federal Farm Loan Act passed

1917   Smith-Hughes Act provides federal aid for teaching vocational subjects in secondary schools
           Literacy test for immigrants adopted

1919   Eighteenth Amendment (Prohibition) ratified
           National Catholic Welfare Council organized

1920   Nineteenth Amendment (Woman Suffrage) ratified

1922   Capper-Volstead Act protects co-operatives from prosecution under the Sherman Antitrust Act

Suggested Reading

Most authors of works about the Populist-Progressive period have adopted the viewpoint of the reformers themselves, namely, that the major development of the era was a revolt against the power and influence of the business community. This is true of such major syntheses as Benjamin P. DeWitt, *The Progressive Movement* (1915); Russell Nye, *Midwestern Progressive Politics* (1951); and Eric Goldman, *Rendezvous with Destiny* (1953). A stimulating analysis in a somewhat different vein is John Chamberlain, *Farewell to Reform* (1932). Richard Hofstadter's highly refreshing essay, *The Age of Reform* (1955), cuts through the ideology of reform and considers the behavior of the American people in the period in a new light. Yet this work must be used with great caution; the author omits the organized labor movement, the role of women, and sectional economic aspirations and presents only meager evidence for his major concept of the "status revolution."

The basic factual data of economic history can be found in relevant pages of Edward C. Kirkland, *A History of American Economic Life* (3d ed., 1951); Fred A. Shannon, *The Farmers' Last Frontier* (1945); and Harold U. Faulkner, *The Decline of Laissez-Faire* (1951). The publications of the Research Center in Entrepreneurial

Suggested Reading

History at Harvard University emphasize more precisely the behavior of businessmen; Thomas C. Cochran's *Railroad Leaders, 1845–1890* (1953) is an outstanding example of many stimulating works published by the Center. A pioneering account of the broad ramifications of industrialization is William Miller and Thomas C. Cochran, *The Age of Enterprise* (1942). The impact of changes in transportation is best described in a work which actually covers the period prior to the Civil War, George R. Taylor, *The Transportation Revolution* (1951). Much attention has been devoted to the role of government in economic growth; an excellent review of this literature, with important original comments by the author, is Robert Lively, "The American System," in the *Business History Review*, XXIX (March, 1955), 81–96. Changes in distribution remain one of the extremely important features of industrialization covered by no systematic treatment; the basic facts, however, can be traced in special chapters devoted to the topic in Harold F. Williamson (ed.), *Growth of the American Economy* (2d ed., 1951).

In the era of "shock," historians have emphasized agrarian reform. John D. Hicks, *The Populist Revolt* (1931), though the classic treatment of that subject, suffers primarily from analyzing economic change through the Populists' own eyes. Two important works have recently pointed in new directions: Carl C. Taylor, *The Farmers Movement, 1620–1920* (1953), places farm unrest in the context of the price-and-market system, and Allan G. Bogue, *Money at Interest* (1955), painstakingly spells out the fact that lending conditions on the frontier were far different from what the Populists contended. The most perceptive account of southern Populism is in C. Vann Woodward, *Tom Watson, Agrarian Rebel* (1938). A suggestive but brief treatment of the patrician revolt is in chapter ii of Eric Goldman's *Rendezvous with Destiny*, cited previously. The growth of organized labor is covered in Selig Perlman,

The Response to Industrialism

A History of Trade Unionism in the United States (1922), and of the National Labor Union, in particular, in Gerald N. Grob, "Reform Unionism: The National Labor Union," *Journal of Economic History*, XIV (Spring, 1954), 126–42. The sense of social cleavage of the decade 1886–96 can be traced most clearly in writings of the time, such as Josiah Strong, *Our Country* (1885), but also useful are such secondary works as John Higham, *Strangers in the Land* (1955), and Henry David, *The History of the Haymarket Affair* (1936). Prevailing social theories are well summarized in Richard Hofstadter, *Social Darwinism in American Thought* (1944); Howard Quint, in *The Forging of American Socialism* (1953), presents an able analysis of Bellamy's impact and of the search for greater social unity. Urban features of the heightened tension of the 1890's have received little systematic treatment. Higham, cited above, and Wallace Davies, *Patriotism on Parade* (1955), cover the super-patriot of the time, and the former presents the best capsule account of the American Protective Association. An especially suggestive treatment of the conflict between labor and agriculture is Seymour Lutzky, "The Reform Editors and Their Press," a doctoral dissertation completed at the State University of Iowa in 1951. Although the political highlights of 1896 can be followed in almost any standard treatment of the period, no one has yet analyzed the more significant upheaval of 1894.

Historians have dealt with a few specific examples of economic organization, but the only major work to suggest its importance as a whole is Kenneth Boulding, *The Organizational Revolution* (1953). The causes or effects of business organization have received little treatment, although detailed accounts of the facts of combination and of federal antitrust policy are plentiful. H. R. Seager and C. A. Gulick, Jr., *Trust and Corporation Problems* (1929), is a good review, and Hans B. Thorelli, *The Federal Antitrust Policy: Origination of an*

Suggested Reading

American Tradition (1955), contains a condensed account of the roots of combination. The source of organized effort among merchants and shippers is equally obscure. W. Z. Ripley, *Railroads: Rates and Regulations* (1912), is a good, traditional introduction to the more formal features of protest and regulation, but the most suggestive account of the economic conditions from which protest sprang and the manner in which it became translated into action, though confined to the background of the Interstate Commerce Act of 1887, is Lee Benson, *Merchants, Farmers, and Railroads* (1955). Theodore Saloutos and John D. Hicks describe general farm organizations in *Midwestern Agrarian Discontent* (1951), but a clearer picture of the background of economic organization, and of the co-operative movement, is in the work of Carl C. Taylor, previously cited. For organized labor, Selig Perlman's work, mentioned previously, can be supplemented with Louis Lorwin, *The American Federation of Labor* (1933). An extremely valuable study is Dallas Lee Jones, "The Wilson Administration and Organized Labor," a doctoral dissertation completed at Cornell University in 1953.

One can obtain the clearest sense of the concern for individual values in chapters iv–vi of Richard Hofstadter's *Age of Reform*, cited previously. The new orientation in religion is traced in Henry May, *Protestant Churches and Industrial America* (1949); Aaron Abell, *The Urban Impact on American Protestantism, 1865–1900* (1943); and Father Ryan's autobiography, *Social Doctrine in Action* (1941). There is no scholarly work covering the extremely influential role of women in reform; yet one can catch a glimpse of their activities and objectives in Rheta Childe Dorr, *What Eight Million Women Want* (1910), and Josephine Goldmark, *Impatient Crusader* (1953), a biography of Florence Kelley. C. Wright Mills, *White Collar* (1951), is the best introduction to the new middle class, while

The Response to Industrialism

George Mowry, *The California Progressives* (1951), chapter iv, draws a picture of the same group's approach to public affairs. There are abundant writings on individual intellectual leaders but little on their behavior as a group. Morton G. White presents in *Social Thought in America* (1949) an account of the change to an inductive, experimental approach in the search for knowledge. C. Wright Mills, in his work cited previously, suggests a systematic approach to the behavior of intellectuals, but a more adequate flavor of their values and activities can be obtained in Arthur Mann, *Yankee Reformers in the Urban Age* (1954), and Benjamin O. Flower, *Progressive Men, Women and Movements of the Past Twenty-five Years* (1914). Chapter vi of Hofstadter's *Age of Reform*, mentioned previously, contains an important account of the impact of organization on the individual. The muckrakers are treated in R. R. Regier, *The Era of the Muckrakers* (1932), and the most complete coverage of the Progressive party is in George Mowry, *Theodore Roosevelt and the Progressive Movement* (1946).

The most perceptive account of the adjustment of immigrants to their new environment is Oscar Handlin, *The Uprooted* (1951); Carl Wittke, *We Who Built America* (1939), is a more factual treatment. John Higham's work, previously cited, is a stimulating story of the response of native Americans to the immigrant tide. The classic work on urban growth is Arthur M. Schlesinger, Sr., *The Rise of the City* (1933), but it has been followed by few attempts to trace the evolution of civic life and the changing types of behavior among urban groups. C. W. Patton describes *The Battle for Municipal Reform* (1940) prior to the twentieth century. For most of the story, however, the reader must turn to personal reminiscences and biographies, such as Tom Johnson, *My Story* (1911); Carter Harrison, Jr., *Stormy Years* (1935); and Louis Geiger, *Joseph W. Folk of Missouri* (1953). Lincoln Steffens reveals the seamy side of urban

Suggested Reading

politics in *The Shame of the Cities* (1904). There are no general treatments of the impact of industrial-urban culture upon rural life. Brief but suggestive elements of this neglected story are in Paul H. Johnstone, "Old Ideals versus New Ideas in Farm Life," in *Farmers in a Changing World* (U.S. Department of Agriculture Yearbook [1940]). The early chapters of Grant McConnell, *The Decline of Agrarian Democracy* (1953), contain an account of the interest of urban groups in scientific agriculture and rural education. The significance of the prohibition movement, one of the most fascinating chapters of American history, is best revealed by Peter Odegard, *Pressure Politics* (1928), a scholarly treatment of the Anti-Saloon League.

The best account of the problems of regional economic growth is in C. Vann Woodward, *Origins of the New South* (1951); there is no similar treatment of the West for the same period. An excellent case study of the effect of northeastern policies on the South is George Stocking, *Basing Point Pricing and Regional Development: A Case Study of the Iron and Steel Industry* (1954). The movement for federal investment in irrigation can be traced in A. B. Darling (ed.), *The Public Papers of Francis G. Newlands* (2 vols., 1932), and in flood control in Arthur D. Frank, *The Development of the Federal Program of Flood Control on the Mississippi River* (1930). The standard treatment of the tariff is F. W. Taussig, *Tariff History of the United States* (8th ed., 1931), but a far better picture of the changing economic politics of tariff-making can be obtained from Clarence Lee Miller, *The States of the Old Northwest and the Tariff, 1867–1888* (1929); Festus Summers, *William L. Wilson and Tariff Reform* (1953); and L. Ethan Ellis, *Reciprocity, 1911: A Study in Canadian-American Relations* (1939). Sidney Ratner, *American Taxation* (1942), is the best history of that subject. Little of a systematic nature is known about the organized economic effort behind the anti-

The Response to Industrialism

trust movement; Hans B. Thorelli, *The Federal Antitrust Policy*, cited previously, is excellent for federal policies and court action but probes little into the economic roots of protest. The greatest insight into that important phase of the question can be acquired from *Report of the Industrial Commission* (57th Cong., 1st sess.), Volume XIII, and from the proceedings of the *Chicago Conference on Trusts, 1899* (1900), and *Proceedings of the National Conference on Trusts and Combinations, 1907* (1908).

The political history of the period can best be traced through biographical material. The main works on Theodore Roosevelt are his own *Autobiography* (1913); Henry Pringle, *Theodore Roosevelt* (1931); and John M. Blum's admirable essay, *The Republican Roosevelt* (1954). Henry Pringle, *The Life and Times of William Howard Taft* (1939), is the most complete account of the Taft administration, while the Wilson administration to 1917 is best covered in Arthur Link, *Woodrow Wilson and the Progressive Era* (1954). Two non-biographical works describe crucial elements of political protest: George Mowry, *Theodore Roosevelt and the Progressive Movement* (1946), and Kenneth W. Hechler, *Insurgency: Personalities and Policies of the Taft Era* (1940). The best treatment of the Socialist party is David Shannon, *The Socialist Party of America* (1955). There are no interpretive accounts of the movement for political reform; the same can be said of the woman suffrage movement, although abundant suggestive information about it can be covered in Carrie C. Catt and N. R. Shuler, *Woman Suffrage and Politics* (1926). Carl B. Swisher, *American Constitutional Development* (2d ed., 1954), contains an interpretation of the role of the Supreme Court.

The literature of American foreign policy is abundant but deals mainly with formal diplomatic relations rather than with the dy-

Suggested Reading

namics of expansion and of co-operation and conflict among peoples. Economic or cultural expansion has not received comprehensive treatment. The new navy is more adequately covered; see, for example, George T. Davis, *A Navy Second to None* (1940). Julius Pratt, *Expansionists of 1898* (1936), describes the emotional and intellectual background of "manifest destiny"; an extremely suggestive approach to the same problem is Richard Hofstadter, "Manifest Destiny and the Philippines," in Daniel Aaron (ed.), *America in Crisis* (1952), pages 173–200. Clarence H. Haring describes the Latin-American reaction to expansion in *South America Looks at the United States* (1928). The standard work on the Far East is A. Whitney Griswold, *The Far Eastern Policy of the United States* (1938), while an admirable treatment of relations with a single area is S. K. Stevens, *American Expansion in Hawaii, 1842–1898* (1945). Three valuable studies of Far Eastern relations which probe behind formal negotiations are Charles S. Campbell, *Special Business Interests and the Open Door Policy* (1951); Charles Vevier, *The United States and China, 1906–1913* (1955); and Fred H. Harrington, *God, Mammon, and the Japanese* (1944), which unfolds an exciting tale of missionary, economic, and political adventure. For relations with Latin America the best work is Samuel F. Bemis, *The Latin American Policy of the United States* (1943). An excellent treatment of the Panama affair is in Dwight C. Miner, *The Fight for the Panama Route* (1940). The most suggestive account of the impact of expansion on the American people is in Robert E. Osgood, *Ideals and Self-Interest in America's Foreign Relations* (1953). See also Fred H. Harrington, "The Anti-Imperialist Movement in the United States, 1898–1900," *Mississippi Valley Historical Review*, XXII (September, 1935), 211–23, and Merle E. Curti, *Peace or War: The American Struggle* (1936).

Index

Index

Individualism: philosophy of, 75–76; and political reform, 92; politics of, 89 ff.

Inland navigation, 57–58

Inland Waterways Commission, 58

Insurgency, 135, 146–48

Intellectuals, attitudes of, 74–75

Interchangeable parts, 10

Interstate commerce clause of the Constitution, 160

Interstate Commerce Commission, 56–57

Iron and steel industry, 8–9

James, Henry, 25

Johnson County, Wyoming, "War," 120–21

Kellogg, Edward, *A New Monetary System*, 34

Kellor, Frances, 103

Knights of Labor, 35–37, 86

Knox, Philander C., 174–76

Labor: attitude toward social justice reform, 85–86; in politics, 146; *see also* American Federation of Labor; Knights of Labor; National Labor Union

La Follette, Robert, 92, 132, 133, 139, 146–48

Latin America, attitude toward United States expansion, 175–76

Lee, Ivy, 54

Liberal Republicans, 27

Literary realism, 91–92

Lochner v. *New York*, 159

Lodge, Henry Cabot, 101

McCormick, Cyrus H., 14

McFarland, J. Horace, 83

McKinley, William, 143–44, 170, 178

Mahan, Alfred T., *The Influence of Sea Power on History*, 165–66, 184

Manifest destiny, 102, 167

Marden, Orison Swett, *Success*, 22

Mass production, 9–10

Materialism: development of, 22–23; opposition to, 25–27, 75–76

Middle class, new, 73–74

Mississippi River flood control, 130–31

Monroe Doctrine, 168–69, 173–74

Morgan, J. P., 51, 52

Morse, Samuel F. B., 7

Muckrakers, 89

Muller v. *Oregon*, 91

Munger, Theodore, *The Freedom of the Faith*, 77

Munn v. *Illinois*, 159

National Association of Manufacturers, 53, 67

National Conference of Social Work, 80, 93

National Consumers' League, 79, 81, 90

National Democratic party, 45

National Farmers' Union, 62–63

National Labor Union, 33–35

National Municipal League, 108

National Progressive Republican League, 147, 155

National Rivers and Harbors Congress, 58

Nationalist clubs, 42

Naturalism, 74

Navy, reform of, 165–66

"New Nationalism," 88

"New South," 124

Newlands Arbitration Act, 87

Newlands Irrigation Act, 130, 157

North American Civic League for Immigrants, 103

Northern Securities Company v. *United States*, 139

Open Door notes, 179–80

"Oregon System," 155–56

Organization, economic, significance of, 69–70

Panama Canal, 170–72

Patrons of Husbandry, 29–30

Index